THE LIFE RECOVERY®

—— WORKBOOK FOR ——

Divorce

A Bible-Centered
Approach for Taking
Your Life Back

STEPHEN ARTERBURN
& DAVID STOOP

Tyndale House Publishers
Carol Stream, Illinois

Visit Tyndale online at www.tyndale.com.

TYNDALE, Tyndale's quill logo, and *Life Recovery* are registered trademarks of Tyndale House Publishers.

The Big Book is a registered trademark of A.A. World Services, Inc.

The Life Recovery Workbook for Divorce: A Bible-Centered Approach for Taking Your Life Back

Cover design by Dan Farrell

Edited by Ellen Richard Vosburg

The author is represented by the literary agency of Alive Literary Agency, 7680 Goddard Street, Suite 200, Colorado Springs, CO 80920, www.aliveliterary.com.

For information about special discounts for bulk purchases, please contact Tyndale House Publishers at csresponse@tyndale.com, or call 1-800-323-9400.

ISBN 978-1-4964-4214-7

Printed in the United States of America

26	25	24	23	22	21	20
7	6	5	4	3	2	1

This workbook is dedicated to every fellow struggler who has had the courage to face the truth about themselves, the humility to abandon their flawed attempts at living, and the willingness to find God's truth and live accordingly.

CONTENTS

The Twelve Steps

1. We admitted that we were powerless over our problems and that our lives had become unmanageable.
2. We came to believe that a Power greater than ourselves could restore us to sanity.
3. We made a decision to turn our wills and our lives over to the care of God.
4. We made a searching and fearless moral inventory of ourselves.
5. We admitted to God, to ourselves, and to another human being the exact nature of our wrongs.
6. We were entirely ready to have God remove these defects of character.
7. We humbly asked God to remove our shortcomings.
8. We made a list of all persons we had harmed and became willing to make amends to them all.
9. We made direct amends to such people wherever possible, except when to do so would injure them or others.
10. We continued to take personal inventory, and when we were wrong, promptly admitted it.
11. We sought through prayer and meditation to improve our conscious contact with God, praying only for knowledge of his will for us and the power to carry it out.
12. Having had a spiritual awakening as a result of these steps, we tried to carry this message to others, and to practice these principles in all our affairs.

The Twelve Steps used in *The Life Recovery Workbook* have been adapted with permission from the Twelve Steps of Alcoholics Anonymous.

INTRODUCTION

He heals the brokenhearted and bandages their wounds. . . .
The Lord's delight is in those who fear him, those who put
their hope in his unfailing love. (Psalm 147:3, 11)

This workbook is about transformation from the pain
and betrayal of divorce to the restoration of life. It's about
walking humbly, righteously, and mercifully with God while
accepting his will. Often amid our pain, we oppose God, argue
with him, plead with him for healing, and methodically cut
other people out of our lives. We end up separated from God
and from the people who care for us. We feel abandoned by all.
The Twelve Steps are a path of finding that humble walk that
leads us out of the self-centered living that led to our divorce to
acceptance and a closer relationship with God.

We will be examining the Twelve Steps individually to consider the challenging spiritual lessons that allow us to move
beyond our compulsions, addictions, and pains. Each step has
a new task for us in our recovery, but none of the steps stand
alone. To effectively move through our bondage to acceptance,
we will work the steps in order. Each step prepares us for the
next one, as we develop a greater sense of openness to God's
plan and purpose in our lives.

The path of recovery involves hard and sometimes painful
work. But it is worth the effort. We see the Twelve Steps as a
path and a process that make us better disciples and more committed followers of Jesus Christ. Honesty, humility, and courage

are vital components of faith that can move us back to a vibrant way of living as a follower of Jesus. Welcome to the journey.

STARTING AND LEADING A GROUP

Recovery is best experienced in the context of a group. Two or more willing people can form a powerful bond as they study and work these steps together. With little effort on your part, your struggles, problems, and hang-ups become a blessing to the group. As you open up, everyone else will feel more free to share from their own lives.

Being the leader of a group is actually quite simple. You can find many books on how to lead a small group, but here's a simple and effective way to do it:

1. Find a location in your home, a church, a workplace, or a school, and obtain permission (if necessary) to form the group.
2. Put up a few flyers announcing the time and place, calling it a divorce support group, recovery group, or Twelve Step group.
3. Show up early, arrange the chairs, make some coffee, and welcome people as they arrive.
4. Start when you say you will start by opening in prayer and by reading the Twelve Steps and the correlating Scriptures.
5. Ask if anyone would like to share for three or four minutes. Don't allow others to "fix" the speaker, and if he or she goes on too long, be sure to enforce the time limit.
6. Make sure everyone has a copy of the workbook. Ask them to study Step One for discussion at the next meeting.
7. End when you say you will end by reading the Lord's Prayer.

8. Be sure that everyone knows where to get a workbook and a *Life Recovery Bible*, if they don't already have one.
9. E-mail us—Stephen Arterburn at sarterburn@newlife.com; David Stoop at drstoop@cox.net—and tell us how it's going.
10. Feel good that you are allowing God to use you.

Please remember that working the steps is an art, not a formula. Most often, it is an individualized process.

God be with you on this journey. We pray that you will find healing, serenity, and peace of mind.

PROFILE

Jim thought he had marriage figured out. He would love his wife, Linda; she would respect him; and they would live happily ever after. Jim struggled to respect women because his mother had cruelly abused him throughout his childhood, hurting him one day but treating him like a prince the next. So in his marriage, Jim just kept on showing love by taking care of everything and controlling everything. Thus, he pushed Linda away, and she resisted his control at every level. But he just kept on "loving" her as he had always done, believing that one day she would come around.

Nothing Linda said or did could alter Jim's course of action. He felt a shift in their marriage, but it was not a good shift. It entered into a new level of separation. Still nothing caused him to rethink what he was doing and how he was treating her.

One day reality showed up at the front door in the form of a process server giving him the notice that Linda was divorcing him. The divorce papers were just the beginning of the nightmare he never imagined. Linda was not just divorcing him; she also informed him that she was leaving him for a mutual acquaintance. Later, he would discover that they had been having an affair for a while.

The final blow was when he discovered that Linda was trying to turn their two daughters against him. Thankfully, her efforts did not work. Jim and Linda's daughters knew their mother had done something wrong. They hated their dad's simplistic love/respect world, and they also knew it had driven a wedge between him and their mother. But none of what he did or who he was justified what their mother had done. They accepted and loved their mother in her brokenness, but they were still closely connected with their father. So they set up a meeting to help him.

At their meeting, Jim's daughters told him that his relationships had been failing for decades because he was stuck in a destructive pattern. His harping on the division between love and respect alienated others. His whole life had been destroyed, but he was still talking and lecturing, rather than feeling and grieving and working through his emotions. He was stuck and had no idea he was emotionally dead.

Jim's arrogance led him to believe that he was still in control and that he could figure out whatever he needed to do to "keep moving forward." Without his daughters, he would have probably stayed on that same track and either lived a lonely, isolated life or broken down emotionally and spiritually one day. Fortunately, Jim did not waste another year of his life.

His daughters shared what they saw in him: narcissism, stubborn resistance, arrogance, and emotional detachment. They convinced him that he needed to surrender all that he had been focused on. They showed him that he had never allowed God to take control of his life. Finally, they convinced him that for anything good or great to happen in his life, he had to admit that he did not have the ability within himself alone to recover from this horrible divorce. He finally admitted that he was powerless and that relying on his own power had been the foundation of his unmanageable life. It was the end of Jim's old way of living and the beginning of his Life Recovery journey.

STEP ONE

We admitted that we were powerless over our problems and that our lives had become unmanageable.

Many people think that the Twelve Steps are only good for those who have an addiction. But they are for anybody who realizes that their life is unmanageable. Divorce is evidence of an unmanageable life. If our lives were totally manageable, we would not be engaging in behaviors and attitudes that prevent us from having a healthy and sustainable relationship with our spouse. Habits and behaviors that destroy our relationships with others are signs of "life unmanageability." When we finally realize we are powerless to solve our own problems, we can begin to move toward healing.

Admitting we are powerless means that we honestly acknowledge that we need someone other than ourselves to be in control and empower us to alter our course. In the process, we discover that we are powerless but not helpless. We have the ability to ask for help. We have the ability to stop doing what has caused us misery. We have the power to see the reality of our lives. We have the power to come out of hiding. Even though we are powerless over our problems, we can understand the results of our choices and actions that led to our problems. At this point, we know that we have to change something.

Our lives can get better, but it will require us to stop what we are currently doing and make changes. This is a sign of strength and experience, not weakness. A football team that is losing at halftime has the option to try to win with a different strategy in the second half. Or they could just continue with the same losing strategy, hoping to wear down the other team. We have choices, and most of us who go through a divorce have made many poor choices because we are powerless to make good choices on our own.

Realizing our powerlessness begins our journey to recovery and finding restoration for our broken lives. We no longer have to use self-effort as the means for our change. We admit that we cannot become good enough, strong enough, or wise enough to lead ourselves to a better life. Self-effort and self-will are not God's will. God wants us to rely on him and his will, and we cannot do that until we give up on ourselves as the source of all good things to come. God is the true source. We will not make room for God until we do what we have done in Step One, but it is not easy.

The Bible gives us this perspective on our own efforts: "I know that nothing good lives in me, that is, in my sinful nature. I want to do what is right, but I can't" (Romans 7:18). This is a tough word to hear, but this was written by the apostle Paul, who lived for Christ, was tortured for Christ, and died for Christ. If Paul was able to say that he did not have what it takes in him to do the right thing, it should not be so difficult for us to admit that limitation also. He had seen the light and talked to Jesus on the road to Damascus (Acts 9:1-19), and he still did not have the power to do what he knew was right. Paul knew he needed the power of God to live for God. But before he got to that knowledge, he had to admit to an astounding limitation. He was powerless on his own.

For recovery to begin, we must admit we do not have power over ourselves or others. We need help. We must start at "I can't do this on my own" to begin the journey through the Twelve Steps. When we admit we are powerless, we come alongside many others who have admitted the same thing before us. Now our lives can open up before us with new possibilities.

QUESTIONS FOR **STEP ONE**

Trapped *Genesis 16:1-15*

1. How is my experience of powerlessness similar to Hagar's? How is it different? How have I tried to escape from the pain related to my divorce?

\
\
\
\

2. What has been my experience of anger in my struggle? What scares me about my anger?

\
\
\
\

3. How have I experienced sadness related to my divorce? What scares me about my sadness?

\
\
\
\

4. What are some of my fears about facing my issues?

\
\
\
\

5. Where can I see God in this process right now?

_____

_____

_____

All Is Darkness _Job 6:2-13_

1. Job is very clear about the pain he is feeling. Describe the pain you're experiencing because of your divorce.

_____

_____

_____

2. In what ways have I felt totally powerless in the divorce?

_____

_____

_____

3. How have I tried to be faithful to God in the midst of the divorce?

_____

_____

_____

4. How can Job's experience help me understand my experience of powerlessness?

_____

_____

_____

Worn Out from Sobbing *Psalm 6:1-10*

1. How does my sadness affect my relationships?

2. In what ways have others misunderstood my feelings?

3. David seems to project his anger onto God. That's why we need to get comfortable expressing our anger in relationships, especially our relationship with God. Anger can be a protest. How have I brought my protest into a relationship?

4. Who in my circle of friends, pastors, or family members would be able to help me restore my confidence in God?

Breaking the Cycle *Ecclesiastes 1:1-18*

1. How have I tried to break the cycle of my pain?

2. What strategies have I relied on when I've tried to break the old patterns of behavior?

_____

_____

_____

3. What prevents me from letting go of my own control and declaring that I am powerless?

_____

_____

_____

Like Little Children *Mark 10:13-16*

1. When I feel powerless, do I feel like a little child? How does that feel?

_____

_____

_____

2. When do I feel most cared for?

_____

_____

_____

3. How does being childlike help me depend on God?

_____

_____

_____

The Paradox of Powerlessness *2 Corinthians 4:7-10*

1. Recall some examples of when you have accepted your own powerlessness and embraced God's powerfulness. Describe them here.

_____

_____

_____

2. How do I respond to trouble?

_____

_____

_____

3. How do I respond to being perplexed?

_____

_____

_____

4. What do I do when it feels like God has abandoned me?

_____

_____

_____

*There is great power in realizing
that we are powerless.*

PROFILE

Shane was a good person. He grew up with good parents in a good home. There was a lot of good in Shane's life: He was young and wealthy, and he had a loving wife, Jackie, and two daughters. Shane's philanthropic organization fed thousands of children throughout the world.

Shane was a big target for the evil influences in the world. When evil took its aim, it hit a bull's-eye. It all began with one little compromise. One day, an invitation popped up on his cell phone to view a sex tape of a famous pop star. His desires to view pornography eventually progressed dramatically to seeing prostitutes.

Shane had become a sex addict; he had to have it, and everything else fell out of his life. At first he faked it with his wife, Jackie, but soon he felt intense contempt for her. He became bitter and angry and blamed her for all of his problems. Eventually, Jackie found a text thread with another woman about meeting up. She also found his pornography stash and some receipts for local hotels.

Jackie was determined to fix Shane by making herself more appealing and available to him by changing her hair, working out more, and buying new clothes. Whenever Shane was in bed, she was there with him, looking better than ever. She did not want to be a victim. She took control and became a force to be reckoned with. She also became hyperspiritual. She was up early to read the Bible and pray. She was doing everything she could do to change this man. She did not want to leave him or divorce him. She wanted to cure him and free him of the terrible burden of guilt and shame. Sadly, for all of her efforts, nothing changed Shane.

Finally, Jackie attended a women's Life Recovery meeting at her church. It was there that she learned of the Twelve Steps. She did not really hear much of what was going on during the meeting because she spent most of the time looking through *The Life Recovery Bible* and going over the Twelve Steps. She was astounded by how much Step One resonated with her. It hit her head-on and in the heart. Nothing she had done had changed anything in Shane. But the greater insight came when she looked at the word "problems." It was obvious that Shane had a problem. No matter what she tried, Shane was backing further and further out of their marriage.

Jackie realized that she had a problem too. She had been trying to fix herself, but she was not the problem. She may have contributed to problems in the marriage, but she made no contribution to his decision to betray her. It was an important insight. The shame she took on herself for his shameful behavior drove her to change her behavior so that he would get better. The more she did that, the more he rejected her.

Jackie recognized that her life had become totally unmanageable. She concluded her problem had been thinking that her home remedy would make everything better and all of the pain would go away. She was trying to control her life. She realized she was intensely angry. Angry at what Shane had done. Angry at God for allowing him to do it. Angry at God for allowing her to marry him. And angry at herself for choosing him and for not knowing what to do.

Jackie realized that Shane was not getting better, and the reality of a divorce became more and more evident. With that realization came more and more fear. The fear along with the shame had been driving her to change herself. Fear and shame flooded her mind, her heart, and her body. She also realized she had another challenge: the task of forgiving Shane's unfaithfulness. But she also knew she had a lot of work to do first.

Toward the end of that first Life Recovery meeting, her thoughts moved away from the first step and onto the second: "We came to believe that a Power greater than ourselves could restore us to sanity." Sanity seemed like a strange word, but there were moments when she felt totally crazy. And when she thought of all she had been doing, all of the efforts that had produced nothing, she realized it was some form of insanity because she was not dealing with her reality.

STEP TWO
We came to believe that a Power greater than ourselves could restore us to sanity.

Jackie was like how a lot of Christians are. They believe Jesus has saved them for all eternity, but they do not believe God will transform them in this life. Like them, Jackie was focused on a God powerful enough to instantly heal her husband. But she was not fully acknowledging that he could heal her, too. She did not doubt that God existed; it was obvious to her that there was a God. She also believed the Bible to be true, and she believed the stories about the miracles that she read there. She knew God was powerful enough to perform those miracles and more. She believed God could do anything, and she had been hard at work until God was ready to do what he could do.

Jackie's amazing wake-up call led her to understand that God could do a great work within her, but she was not trusting God to lead her. She was instead led by her two higher powers of shame and fear. The harder she worked under her own power, the greater the shame and fear. She would have to do things in a different way, with a different motive, focused on a different outcome, led not by her own power but by the God of the universe who had far more power than she could even partly understand. And she realized that the more she relied on her own self-will, her own home remedies of control and manipulation, the less opportunity God had to use his power in her life.

Jackie went from knowing conceptually that God had the power to do anything and everything to believing God had the power to help her with her biggest problem: herself. And she believed God was already at work on Shane. But for now, she had come to believe that God could, wanted to, and would restore her to sanity if she would stop trying to do everything herself and trust him for all her problems. God could do it, but she would need to cooperate.

Jackie looked at the verse that goes with Step Two and fully believed it was the basis for all she had come to accept at that meeting: "God is working in you, giving you the desire and the power to do what pleases him" (Philippians 2:13). She fully believed that God was working in her. During that powerful Life Recovery meeting, God had sparked a new desire to do what pleased him.

As you work through the questions that follow, be sure you have admitted and accepted that your power on its own has not produced change. Also, be sure you are focused on the right problem: you. This is not about a conceptual God out to make the universe a better place. Step Two is about truly believing that the God of the universe loves you, has not abandoned you, and has some very good things for you, including restoration, recovery, and sanity.

QUESTIONS FOR **STEP TWO**

Persistent Seeking *Job 14:1-6*

1. What are my objections to trusting God fully with my life?

_____

_____

_____

2. What emotions and questions do I need to share with God, honestly?

_____

_____

_____

3. Am I willing to work through the pain and unfairness in my life in order to find God and be freed from the obsessive questioning and thoughts? What holds me back?

_____

_____

_____

Grandiose Thinking *Daniel 4:19-33*

1. How do I display the belief that I am only accountable to myself in my behavior?

_____

_____

_____

2. How have I tried to have power over the events, outcomes, and people in my life?

_____

_____

_____

3. In what ways do I still show that I have forgotten that God is ultimately in control?

_____

_____

_____

Internal Bondage *Mark 5:1-13*

1. What self-destructive behaviors have I been tempted to do? List and describe them.

_____

_____

_____

2. How have my obsessive fears about the future kept me from living in the present? In what ways have I been more comfortable living in tombs of isolation and silent judgment?

_____

_____

_____

3. What motivated me to come to believe that I needed to rely on Jesus?

_____

_____

_____

Healing Faith *Luke 8:43-48*

1. How have I tried to control my life situation in my own power? What were the results?

_____

_____

_____

2. Am I ready to reach out to Jesus as my Higher Power? Write a note to God about your readiness.

_____

_____

_____

Believe *Romans 1:18-20*

1. What experiences have I had that have shown me that self-sufficiency is not the way I want to live?

_____

_____

_____

2. How have I seen God's power at work in other people's lives? How can those examples be an encouragement to me as I wait to see God work in my life?

_____

_____

_____

3. What are the signs that I am in the process of being restored to sanity?

_____

_____

Rejoice Always *Romans 5:3-11; James 1:2*

1. How do I think powerlessness relates to my being able to rejoice in the midst of my troubles?

_____

_____

_____

2. When I accept my powerlessness and can rejoice in the midst of my pain, what do Paul and James say will be the result?

_____

_____

_____

An Overwhelming Struggle *Romans 8:35-39*

1. Sometimes we feel like giving up the struggle of accepting our own powerlessness. What should I do when those times come?

   _____

   _____

   _____

2. How does it help me in my struggle to realize that God loves me no matter what?

   _____

   _____

   _____

3. What does knowing that God cares about my marital status mean to me?

   _____

   _____

   _____

Hope in Faith *Hebrews 11:1-10*

1. Am I able to believe that God can help me to live free of my compulsions? How?

   _____

   _____

   _____

2. Can I now believe, as I reach out for God's strength and surrender to him, that it is God's nature to be present and ready to help? Why or why not?

   _____

   _____

   _____

Faith begins when we believe that God is who he says he is.

PROFILE

The names *Carl* and *Carla* sound nice together, but their wedding was the beginning of a complete disaster. Carl and Carla thought their names might be a sign from God that they were meant to be together and eventually married. After dating for six months, and not really knowing each other well, they were married by a justice of the peace; an ironic title, justice of the peace, because shortly after that officer of the court completed the process, the fighting began.

Five years later that same court was processing divorce papers, receiving abuse claims, issuing protective orders, and eventually granting full custody of the two children to Carl. Their life together all seemed so perfectly wonderful in the beginning, but it turned out to be so horrifically sad in the end. No one would have predicted the outcome, but problems surfaced quickly. Having kids only added more pressure and exacerbated all of the issues that eventually led to the divorce.

From Carla's perspective, Carl stopped paying attention to her immediately after they were married. She was vulnerable when her boss paid her special attention and finally seduced her into an affair. Their relationship eventually led to them moving in together. Rather than spend thousands of dollars trying to win custody of the children, she allowed Carl to keep them in the home where they were growing up. She said she was sacrificing her rights so that they would not be inconvenienced going back and forth between the two parents. She would see them every other weekend and on Wednesdays. That was how she saw life going forward into a new future—almost as if Carl and Carla and the kids had never existed.

From Carl's perspective, immediately after they were married, Carla became a person he had never met. It was a nightmare of a marriage. Carl felt criticized all the time. Nothing he did well brought praise, and everything else brought a nasty comment. It felt as if she had lured him into marriage and then showed him who she really was all along. So he did everything in his power to flip her back to the person he thought he married. He did all the housework, brought her gifts, and tried to please her. But nothing made it better, and he quickly ran out of any desire to fix it.

The worse their relationship grew, the more he drank. More than enough was never enough, so he went from doing all he could to please her to drinking as much as pleased himself. Severe alcoholism seemed to come on instantly, which made everything worse for him and Carla. At the end of their fourth year of marriage, she filed for divorce, and this was Carl's wake-up call. The next day was the first day with no alcohol in his system. He started going to meetings and therapy and fairly quickly came to his senses and was working a solid recovery program, including working the Twelve Steps.

Once Carl learned the Twelve Steps and was on the road to recovery for his alcoholism, he then turned his focus to working the steps for his divorce. The circumstances of his . divorce were all evidence that his life was out of control and full of insanity. He worked to truly believe God would help him if he surrendered to God's power and will. Carl made the decision to turn his life over to God in this area, just as he had turned his life over to God in the area of drinking. Carl then experienced a serenity he had thought would never be possible.

Surrender is never easy. Trying to control what cannot be controlled is much harder and intensifies all of the destructive emotions that emerge from turmoil and ineffective efforts. Carl was full of anger and bitterness over so many elements of his life. The third step did not resolve all of Carl's anger or fears or despair, but it did help him work toward resolving those emotions and move toward sanity and serenity. The remaining steps would take him the rest of the way.

STEP THREE

We made a decision to turn our wills and our lives over to the care of God.

Deciding is a powerful act. It replaces wishing or waiting for a miracle to change everything back to the way it was. Deciding to stop fighting and to start living for a caring God is the most powerful choice we can make. Before we surrender, we usually do all sorts of research. We see how much our own power can manage things, and we manage to make everything worse. We try harder only to discover we cannot try hard enough. We are dying spiritually, emotionally, and even physically due to failed attempts to control the outcome. Fortunately, our dying leads us toward surrender to God.

When we turn our wills over to God, we are surrendering our self-will to God's will. The obvious question then is, "What is God's will for me?" When we ask that we are usually thinking about a very defined path toward a very defined outcome that we hope we like. There is no defined path, because life is not without twists and turns brought about by fallible people living in a fallen world, making choices that hurt themselves and others. Unexpected things happen along the way. Rather than try to define the destination or plot the perfect path, we can live God's will one choice at a time. It is simply stopping long enough to make a choice to do the next right thing.

What a relief that when we accept that God is in control, we can start to live one day at a time, one hour at a time, one choice at a time. We don't have to worry about how difficult and complex our lives may become, because we have put them in God's hands. In God's hands, we search for what is good, true, responsible, and right. We do that and let God handle the rest while we live in the comfort and security of knowing God is there for us as we make tough choices that honor him.

This choice to surrender to God comes with many complications. The shameful things we have done have often caused us to wonder when God is going to swoop in and punish us. We don't want to be closer to God; we want to run away because we have come to believe that God is angry or will discipline us torturously or does not even care for us. Additionally, there are some bad people who have not represented God well. They have abused or controlled or hurt people in the name of God. If we equate them with God or godly living, we will have a difficult time surrendering to God.

Deciding to turn our wills and our lives over to the care of God does not mean that we wait for God to act while we do nothing. It is not a decision to retreat; it is a choice to take action with God. The choices will be difficult in the short term but will have long-term benefits. We are not just sitting around as helpless and hopeless failures passively living in God's love. We are instead actively engaged with God in the transformation of our lives, which requires hard work and some discomfort. With God's help and power, the comfort—or serenity and sanity—returns as we come to believe in a hopeful future. But first, we must surrender to the God who has the power we do not have. We choose God, and in so doing we choose recovery, restoration, and healing.

QUESTIONS FOR **STEP THREE**

Trusting God *Numbers 23:18-24*

1. What in my life has taught me to distrust God?

_____

_____

_____

2. What have I done to cause others to distrust me?

_____

_____

_____

3. What really keeps me from surrendering to God?

_____

_____

_____

It's Your Choice *Deuteronomy 30:15-20*

1. What is it about my understanding of God that blocks me from deciding to turn my life and my will over to his care?

_____

_____

_____

2. How does fear affect my choices?

_____

_____

_____

Doing God's Will *1 Samuel 24:1-11*

1. Can I remember a situation when I knew what God wanted me to do, but I did what I wanted to do? Describe that time here.

_____

_____

_____

2. David had surrendered his will to God's will. What is God's will in reference to my divorce? Have I fully surrendered my will to God's? How is God's will different from my will?

_____

_____

_____

3. Share an example of when doing God's will was difficult.

_____

_____

_____

Giving Up Control *Psalm 61:1-8*

1. Where did I get the illusion that I can control other people, my circumstances, my job, or my life?

_____

_____

_____

2. What stops me from surrendering my will and my life so that I can find the life God intends for me?

_____

_____

_____

Redeeming the Past *Isaiah 54:4-8*

1. Do I tend to hold God at arm's length? Why?

_____

_____

_____

2. What fears have the most power in my life?

_____

_____

_____

3. How is shame connected to my fears?

_____

_____

_____

God Is Faithful *Lamentations 3:17-26*

1. What in my circumstances at this point makes it hard for me to believe God is faithful?

_____

_____

_____

2. Which hopes and dreams of mine have been crushed?

_____

_____

_____

3. As Jeremiah grieves over fallen Jerusalem, he reminds himself of God's faithfulness. What can I call to mind that reminds me of God's faithfulness?

_____

_____

_____

Submission and Rest *Matthew 11:27-30*

1. Why do I think I can handle some of my divorce issues on my own with no other help?

_____

_____

_____

2. What do I need to do to be ready to learn from others?

_____

_____

_____

3. What aspects of my personality prevent me from listening to and learning from Jesus?

_____

_____

_____

Discovering God *Acts 17:22-28*

1. How would I define the word *surrender*?

_____

_____

_____

2. How would I differentiate between "my will" and "my life"?

_____

_____

_____

There comes a point at which we can either merely have faith or make a bold move and really live our faith. When we live our faith, we no longer just talk about our beliefs, our lives reflect them: What I believe and say and do all line up. But this alignment only happens when we have enough faith to turn everything over to God—every compartment, every hidden secret, everything—and acknowledge, perhaps for the very first time, that God is the Highest Power in our lives.

PROFILE

Terri felt like she had married a fraud. While they were dating, Daniel had lavished money and fancy trips upon her. They had traveled the world together. But once they were married, the money was gone along with Daniel's sense of adventure. His life suddenly consisted only of going to work and coming home to sit in his favorite chair. Soon, Daniel was cheating on Terri with many other women.

However, Terri might never have made the move to divorce him if he had not divorced her. She had begged that they get help, but he was unwilling. Then Daniel found someone about half his age, moved in with her, and divorced Terri as quickly as he could. Essentially, he left Terri with nothing. He had even manipulated her into sharing an attorney, which turned out horribly for Terri. Terri was left barely hanging on to her faith in God and with a whole lot of resentment.

Terri became obsessed with complaining about her divorce, which eventually alienated her friends. She also quit seeing two different counselors who encouraged her to examine her own mistakes that led to her divorce. That was something she was not willing to do, and she thought it was evidence of bad counseling. To her, Daniel was so terrible that she did not need to look at her own issues. Three years went by before she was willing to do any self-examination because it was too painful.

Three years postdivorce, Terri was still in deep pain. She was severely stuck and could not move on. The trauma of betrayal and divorce had left her bitter. Life and work became more and more difficult. She fell into a severe depression. If it were not for medication, she would not have been able to function. The medication allowed her to keep functioning through her daily life, but it did something else, too. It opened a window of insight into the reality of who she had become and what she was doing with her life. She was allowing her obsession over the man who hurt her so deeply to destroy her, and she didn't want to allow that anymore. When Terri's counselor asked her again if she thought it was time for her to look at her life and do some work that could result in her living life in a different way, she agreed it was time. Their next session was the beginning of Terri's healing.

Terri was led by her counselor to attend her first Life Recovery meeting that focused on codependency. Her counselor told her it was an important first step toward the hope for healing. When she attended, she learned about the concept of "my side of the street." The concept was that she needed to work on her own problems rather than focus on what was wrong with someone else. She accepted the need to work on herself by attending the meetings, getting a sponsor, working the steps, and gaining some much-needed insight from her counselor. Consistently sticking with this simple program resulted in Terri coming to grips with her reality, putting Daniel and her life with him in the past, and moving on. The journey out of her misery required her to work the first three steps, but it was Step Four that required her to explore and search rather than deny and distract herself from her pain and state of helplessness.

STEP FOUR

We made a searching and fearless moral inventory of ourselves.

The first three steps produced a radical change in perspective. We experienced a life-changing move away from thinking we have what it takes to realizing we do not. In the absence of the false belief that we have the power we need, we became open to the prospect that there is a God who cares about us and has all of the power we need. Then, we made a very humbling choice to surrender and turn everything over to this almighty God, whom we have come to believe can do anything, and with our cooperation, he will enable us to work through our problems. Once that work is done, we can continue working Steps Four through Twelve. Step Four is a step toward acceptance.

Acceptance is the answer to all of our problems. We cannot change reality unless we accept it. The problem with acceptance is that we cannot accept what we do not see. Step Four helps us see some very important issues that we may have been overlooking, ignoring, or denying. Sometimes we refuse to see these issues because the pain seems too great. But at some point, we have to look and see, understand and accept.

Taking an inventory of ourselves requires patience, courage, and willingness. We have to become willing to take a look at many things we would prefer not to face. We must search for truth that is not tainted by shame or distorted by defensive justification. In simple terms, we must look honestly at what we have, what we have done with it, and the impact of it on others.

Perhaps the most defining word of this step is *moral*. *Moral* carries with it the concept of right and wrong. Godly choices are moral choices. Ungodly behavior is immoral. So if we are to conduct a moral inventory, we have to look back and say that everything we did was not okay, nor was everything that was done to us. There are so many voices that want us to believe there is no ultimate right or definitive wrong, but we know the difference. We felt it when we did it, and we felt it when it was done to us.

A holy God is worthy of our self-examination to determine

what we did right and what we did wrong. Examining ourselves can be painful, but it is so much better than trying to act like nothing ever happened. Two of the greatest tools toward recovery and healing are a notebook and a pen. Writing our struggles down is cathartic and helps us face reality. If hurtful things from the past are on paper, we may feel less need to go over and over them in our heads.

When working this vital step, there are some things that could be helpful to consider: Where and when and how have we been hurt? Who caused pain in our lives, and how did we respond to it? What conclusions were formed about others or what vows were made to protect ourselves? Who have we hurt or been irresponsible with? What was the impact of our behavior on them? Where were the inconsistencies between image and behavior? How was a double life maintained? Who did we walk on or over? What destructive behaviors are still present in our lives?

People, organizations, events, and our own choices form the foundations of our defects that separate us from God and leave us feeling isolated from others. It can be surprising and shocking to see the evidence of our brokenness. But facing it head-on allows us to accept who we are, what we have been through, and what we need to do to recover and heal.

QUESTIONS FOR **STEP FOUR**

Coming Out of Hiding Genesis 3:6-13

1. When and how have I led a "double life," trying to look good while full of shame on the inside about my life?

_____

_____

_____

2. In what ways has shame taken root in my heart?

_____

_____

_____

3. Am I ready to deal with "the dirt" so I can live free? What holds me back?

_____

_____

_____

Enter into the Sadness _Nehemiah 8:7-10_

1. What painful memories keep me from going forward in writing my Step Four inventory? Describe them.

_____

_____

_____

2. What am I afraid of facing?

_____

_____

_____

3. What role has shame from past mistakes played in keeping me from starting and completing an inventory?

_____

_____

_____

4. How does pride play into my hiding?

_____

_____

_____

Confession _Nehemiah 9:1-3_

1. What behaviors over my lifetime have been offensive to God?

_____

_____

_____

2. What destructive habits do I need to confess to God?

_____

_____

_____

3. What keeps me from being honest with God?

_____

_____

_____

4. What consequences from past wrong choices am I still living with today?

_____

_____

_____

It's All in the Family *Nehemiah 9:14-38*

1. Are there family members or friends with whom I need to make things right? Name them here.

_____

_____

_____

2. What unfinished business do I need to face with my family or friends as part of my inventory?

_____

_____

_____

Handling Anger *Matthew 5:21-26*

1. Is my fear of becoming angry holding me back from taking my inventory?

_____

_____

_____

2. The real danger in becoming angry is in venting my anger in unhealthy or harmful ways. Can I be angry and not vent in ways that lead me further from my goal?

_____

_____

_____

3. In this passage in Matthew, Jesus teaches about making things right so that we can have reconciliation. We will make things right at Step Nine. Will I be able to wait to

make things right until then? Include these considerations in your inventory.

_____

_____

_____

_____

Finger-Pointing _Matthew 7:1-5_

1. Is it easier to look at the faults and shortcomings of other people in my life, past and present, than to recognize my own?

_____

_____

_____

_____

2. What is the "log" in my eye, the blind spot that has caused trouble and given rise to pride, finger-pointing, and eventually my chaotic life?

_____

_____

_____

_____

3. Where and when have I stepped on people's toes and invited retaliation? Have I been proud, blaming, or fearful?

_____

_____

_____

_____

Constructive Sorrow *2 Corinthians 7:8-11*

1. In what ways have I avoided facing my sorrow about how my divorce has impacted my life and the lives of others?

_____

_____

_____

_____

2. Have I been willing to set aside time to grieve and to allow humility to grow in me? What stops me?

_____

_____

_____

_____

3. Have I also been self-condemning? What blocks me from experiencing God's grace?

_____

_____

_____

_____

God's Mercy *Revelation 20:1-15*

1. Taking a moral inventory of myself here on earth will help to prepare me for the life to come. How do I still resist making an inventory?

_____

_____

_____

2. As I trusted God in Step Three, am I able to let go of my pride and fear in Step Four and allow his will to be expressed through me? If so, write out a prayer of trust and willingness to complete Step Four.

_____

_____

_____

_____

_____

_____

_____

_____

_____

3. Write down a list and description of fears, resentments, wrongdoings, and character flaws.

Fears:

_____

_____

Resentments:

_____

_____

Wrongdoings (actions I have committed that oppose God's standards):

_____

_____

Character flaws (remember that honesty and humility are character strengths that you are building here, so be as thorough and honest as possible to move toward long-term recovery):

_____

_____

4. After careful self-examination, am I more convinced than ever that I need a Savior every day, not just for salvation but to walk in freedom from sin? If so, write out a prayer to God that expresses your complete dependence upon him for salvation and freedom.

_____

_____

_____

_____

_____

_____

_____

_____

In Psalm 119:29, the writer pleads with God: "Keep me from lying to myself." Our inventory, when compiled with honesty and diligence, is the beginning of facing the truth about our need to grow in character and maturity, in spite of our losses. It is welcoming the new, authentic self.

PROFILE

Mark and Becky had so much going for them from the very beginning. They were high school sweethearts who were voted homecoming king and queen. They went to medical school together and opened a pediatric practice together. They achieved great success and were able to live a financially secure lifestyle. They were a popular couple, and they loved their life together. It was all too good to be true. But after twenty years of marriage, the problems began to show.

Mark said it was boredom that led to the problem. They were so successful that the security and predictability became a bit of a negative. Eventually, they developed a routine of working together but relaxing apart. For a while that meant doing different things once at home. Then Becky decided she needed to get away by herself. Some might have called it separate vacations, but they chose not to go public with their growing desire not to be together.

On the other hand, Becky said that the problem was that Mark bugged her most of the time. The predictability that bothered her was how predictably arrogant and controlling he was. He was critical and demanding at the office, as if they were not married partners or equal partners in their practice. He controlled every cent and tried to control her, too. She felt that he suffocated their love, their marriage, and her spirit.

Becky took a month off by herself in the south of France

and did quite a bit of thinking. France was full of romance and beauty, and she felt so free and lighthearted. When she returned, she was inspired to file for divorce. Mark thought he could control that also, but he was wrong. He was devastated about dividing up all that he had counted on for his safe retirement—he had become that cold and uncaring toward his wife. So Mark and Becky divorced after months of working with attorneys to split up the practice and the rest of their lives.

It was about six months after the divorce that Mark started to realize he had never been more miserable in his life. And it was about nine months after the divorce that he started to realize he was the source of his misery. He continued to have little glimpses of truth and insights into what he had been doing and the impact it had on others, but he wasn't sure what to do.

Around this same time, a new dentist moved to town and decided to befriend Mark. Mark was too busy for friends, but the new dentist persisted in calling, and they had coffee a couple of times. When he heard about Mark's divorce, he suggested that Mark attend a Life Recovery group for those who have been through a divorce. He said he would pick him up and go with him. When they went, the group was on Step Five. After he heard the positive impact working Step Five had on so many there, Mark was determined to work Steps One through Four so he could get to Five.

When Mark had finished working Step Five, it did not save his marriage, but it did save him from a lifetime of resentment and isolation. It saved him from years of feeling shame and isolation, denial and superficiality. In many ways, it felt like the beginning of his life of freedom and rich connection with others. Mark discovered that openness leads to healing and deception leads to sickness. He completed his inventory, and then he admitted all that he had discovered and realized to God, to himself, and to one of the members of the Life Recovery group. The weight of the burden of shame began to lift immediately.

STEP FIVE

We admitted to God, to ourselves, and to another human being the exact nature of our wrongs.

My (Steve's) friend Dave has said for years that he does not want to die before he is dead. It is a profound concept, and I share it with him. We both want to be full of life and live it to the fullest up to the last moment possible. Shame kills living. Secrecy cuts us off from the life we were created to experience. Openness changes everything. Confession moves us out of isolation and alienation and brings us back to life. If we are used to a life of silence and secrecy, confession can be one of the most difficult things we ever do.

Confessing the truth starts with a willingness to admit the truth to ourselves. We may have had a story that we told ourselves that rationalized or justified everything we have ever done. Hopefully in working Step Four we walked away from the myths we created and embraced the reality before us. Writing it out has helped us see it and accept it, but we must not just accept the facts of our defects and shortcomings. We must accept the need to open up to God and someone else after we have admitted to ourselves that what we have written is true.

The psalmist said his "bones waxed old" in his silence (Psalm 32:3, KJV). He was getting sicker the longer he held in what he needed to get out. Our shame keeps us from opening up. We are driven by fear of what will happen when the shameful things of our lives are known. We are afraid of being judged and rejected when someone else finds out about our problems. But in this step, we are not about to broadcast to the whole world what we have done. It is between God and ourselves and one other person. It is important that the person we open up to is the right person. We want to be open with someone who is safe and trustworthy. Depending on our situation, that person could be a therapist, a pastor, or a sponsor. A sponsor is the natural choice for hearing what we write out in Step Four. Choosing the person who will hear about our shortcomings wisely can provide the freedom to disclose what we have destructively kept silent.

Shame leads to the fear that encourages us to keep our secrets concealed. Pride will do the same thing. Believing we are above everyone else will stop our willingness to open up. Humility brings us down to the level of everyone else and removes our reasons to hide. Humility moves us into an authentic desire to do the next right thing. It also puts the self in the proper perspective. It is not our job to protect ourselves from others knowing who we really are. We have a God-given mission to use the painful events from our past to help others. We won't do that if our goal is image-protection and self-preservation. This fifth step is a powerful way to move out of the role of self-preservation and into the role of fellow healer.

One of the most powerful things we do in this step is ask God for forgiveness in the presence of someone else. At the conclusion of your time of confession, it might be good to pray together for a few minutes a simple prayer such as this one:

> God, you have heard all of the character defects I can recall. You know I need help so I can learn and grow from all that is in my past. Please forgive me for my wrongdoings. Please forgive me for rebelling against you and hurting others. I ask you to forgive me and comfort those who suffered because of my mistakes. Thank you for your forgiveness. Amen.

The freedom from shame that comes from the combination of opening up to another person and at the same time asking God to forgive us goes a long way in protecting ourselves from ever making the same mistakes again.

Opening ourselves up to God and another person is one of the greatest acts of courage anyone can do. Revealing what we have been intent on hiding takes a huge burden from our hearts. Deception is thrown away and replaced with a desire to be known, loved, and accepted. Because the shift in mood and motivation can be so profound, a person could decide they have leapt into mental health and stability. We must not forget this is Step Five out of twelve. While the impact of this step can be profound, we need to continue to do the work of all Twelve Steps so that the impact of working Step Five is not just a fleeting moment of relief. It needs to be a huge step into mature living where we are free to be open and share our authentic selves.

QUESTIONS FOR **STEP FIVE**

Overcoming Denial *Genesis 38:1-30*

1. What am I avoiding in Step Four by delaying Step Five?

_____

_____

_____

2. What is the exact nature of my wrongs as listed in my fear-less moral inventory?

_____

_____

_____

3. Why am I afraid to have someone hear my confession of my inventory?

_____

_____

_____

4. What interferes with my being honest about myself?

_____

_____

_____

Crying Out to God   _Psalm 38:9-16_

1. To some people, divorce is like a disease. They are afraid of it. Has anyone withdrawn from me because they believed that? How did that make me feel?

_____

_____

_____

_____

2. Have I felt abandoned by friends or family members because of my divorce? What do I do with my feelings of abandonment?

_____

_____

_____

_____

3. How do I keep focused on God, who always understands the pain of my shame?

_____

_____

_____

_____

Joyful Confession *Isaiah 43:25–44:5*

1. In what ways does my life feel like a parched field?

   _____

   _____

   _____

   _____

2. In what ways have I neglected to feed my spirit?

   _____

   _____

   _____

   _____

3. In what ways have I experienced God's longing to replenish my life?

   _____

   _____

   _____

   _____

4. Have I set the appointment for completing Step Five by sharing my Step Four inventory?

   My commitment to myself:

   Date:

   Time:

   Who:

   _____

   _____

Covenant Love *Hosea 11:8-11*

1. How do I react to the truth that God does not give up on me?

_____

_____

_____

2. What keeps me from being truthful with God?

_____

_____

_____

3. What makes me think I can hide anything from God?

_____

_____

_____

The Plumb Line *Amos 7:7-8*

1. Have my morals and values been in line with God's? Explain.

_____

_____

_____

2. Where have I had difficulty applying my morals and values in my life?

_____

_____

_____

3. What has kept me from staying in line with God's morals and values?

_____

_____

_____

4. Am I ready to surrender to God's moral plumb line? If not, why am I hesitating?

_____

_____

_____

Healing through Confession _James 5:16-18_

1. How do I still resist confessing my inventory to another person?

_____

_____

_____

2. How do I react to the fact that it isn't enough to confess to God alone?

_____

_____

_____

3. Make a decision: To whom will I read my inventory?

_____

_____

A great weight is lifted when we confess.

PROFILE

Jenna was raised in a home where anger was far more prevalent than love. Her father was an extremely angry man who often lashed out at Jenna and her four sisters, verbally and physically. They were afraid of his outbursts that would often lead to what he called a spanking but was much more like a beating.

As Jenna grew up, she had some difficulty with trusting God. If God was anything like her father, she knew he was not happy with her, and it was only a matter of time before his wrath came her way. She was a Christian, but her relationship with God was distant and tainted by the experiences she had with her own father. Jenna felt like she needed to be perfect so her father would not yell at her or punish her, and she thought God worked the same way.

Eventually, Jenna met Danny, and they had a fairly normal courtship that lasted a year and an engagement that lasted six months. They bonded most over their shared passion for outdoor adventure. They were constantly on the go and enjoying life as they approached their wedding date. Jenna was quite emotional at times, but her behavior didn't seem alarming or out of the ordinary to Danny. He had no idea what was ahead.

Shortly after they married, they did not have as much time to be outdoors as they once did. Both of them worked hard all week, and their weekends became less about adventure and more about rest, recovery, and getting ready for the work-week. This new dynamic seemed to change their relationship altogether. Jenna found herself more and more irritated with Danny. To Danny's amazement, within six months Jenna was acting just like her father.

In the beginning he thought it was a phase that would go away, but instead it intensified. She shouted and raged and railed against anything Danny did. He felt like he could do no right. He begged her to get some help, and she thought that was just another sign of his weakness. She could not see what she was doing, and it was destroying Danny and their marriage. He tried being the nice guy, the compliant guy, and the pleaser guy. None of that worked, so he tried the opposite. He tried being the tough guy, the distant guy, and the guy in charge. No matter what he did, it did not change her and only increased his despair.

While Jenna had quickly shifted into this state of anger and total dissatisfaction, Danny was even more sudden in his move. One day Danny woke up, called and met with an attorney, and filed for divorce. He also rented an apartment and moved out. All in the same day. Within ninety days, he had divorced Jenna. Jenna could not believe what had happened. She knew he was not happy anymore, but she never thought he would move out or divorce her. It was such a shock that it forced her to look at what she had done, how she had treated him, and how he had become so miserable so quickly.

A friend recommended that Jenna attend a Life Recovery meeting at a local church to get some support and gain some insight into what her contribution to the divorce was. That was where she first encountered the Twelve Steps. She began working through them with a sponsor she met at the first meeting. Through the steps she saw how her own efforts to fix things like Danny or their marriage had made things worse. She worked Step Four and wrote down the things that she could see that were problems for her. She willingly opened up about them to her sponsor. But when she came to Step Six, she hit a wall that took her a couple of years to knock down because she was not entirely ready to change or do what it would take to get rid of all of her ways of handling things.

They had some benefits she did not want to part with. But she never gave up on God, and God did not give up on her. After two years, she was entirely ready to cooperate with God.

STEP SIX

We were entirely ready to have God remove these defects of character.

Step Six may not seem like it would be very difficult, or some might think it is not needed, but it is a valuable pause in the action of recovery. It is a step that invites us to ask whether or not we are truly entirely ready for God to do a major work in our lives. Some people want to keep trying harder at what they've done in the past. This can be a key part of getting entirely ready because when you do keep doing what has not worked in the past, more effort doing it usually leads to more of the same bad results. Once you go through that cycle a time or two, you might find yourself entirely ready to start cooperating with God under his power rather than yours. A better path is to become entirely ready without having to go through any more cycles of failure.

When we are entirely ready for God to remove our defects of character, it means a few very important things. It means we are no longer just in compliance mode. Compliance is a whole lot better than resistance, but it is not a state of being entirely ready for God to work. Compliance can result in regular attendance at meetings but not really being engaged with what is happening. It can mean reading the recovery literature but not applying it to real life. Compliance looks good on the outside, but inside there is little transformation going on. It becomes another form of the duplicity we have been living out with our secret obsessions, compulsions, habits, and poor choices, while presenting images of strength and responsibility. It is a place far from being entirely ready.

When we are entirely ready for God to take over and remove our character defects, we have humbled ourselves and recognized our limitations, and we want God's unlimited power to be at work in our lives. We're done with superficial living that has left us empty and looking ridiculous to those who really know us. We have no desire to attempt to create or preserve false images or live inconsistently from our public self. We seek congruency and authenticity over faking anything any longer. Being entirely ready means we can meet who we are and be who we are, no matter how uncomfortable it is or the consequences it creates. It is a "less of me, more of God" attitude in all things. It is a willingness to painfully strip away what we have painfully struggled to maintain and allow God full access to our hearts.

Being entirely ready requires an examination of our motives. Motives such as power, control, image-maintenance, and pain-avoidance are replaced by wanting to find purpose and meaning in redemptive relationships with God and others. We become so motivated by finding the right path and making things right with others that we are ready for anything we need to do to allow God to have control of our lives.

Once we become entirely ready, we can almost be assured that our readiness will be challenged. We will be tempted to follow the paths of others who have less sincere motives. We will question what we have done and whether or not the pain of it all is worth it. Our fears will arise, and the words of others may stoke the fear flames in our hearts. Shame may arise to cause us to question God's desire to do something with us or in us. Regrets of the past and fears of the future will blend together in attempts to shackle us so that we cannot do the next right thing or take the next right step. We will succumb to the forces that rise up against us unless we are tethered to supportive people involved in our recovery. We will need a close sponsor to help us rein in the negative and persevere. Scripture tells us that those who persevere obtain the crown of life. They also obtain a deep and meaningful trust relationship with the only one who can grant that crown.

A final note on readiness: Readiness must mean active cooperation rather than passively waiting for God to do what God is waiting for us to do. Wishing with false hope is far from willing cooperation to get a little better and do a little better each day. And what is the focus of our readiness? Our defects of character. We have them, and we must continue to search for them and accept them and be ready for God to work with us to remove them. If we are still in a place where we feel we are better than others and have little work to be done on any defects, then we are not ready at all. The Bible also tells us that everyone has sinned and fallen short of God's standard (Romans 3:23). None of us is an exception. We are all in this together. Those who become entirely ready to have God remove their defects of character are the ones who recover, restore, and redeem all of their pain and suffering. They find the power to change and transform in the only one who has the power to change and transform. That power leads them one step at a time to becoming redemptive forces in the world.

If you are entirely ready, the questions below will help you grow deeper in your desire to restore what has been broken.

QUESTIONS FOR **STEP SIX**

Taking Time to Grieve *Genesis 23:1-4; 35:19-21*

1. What is standing in the way of my being able to allow God to remove my shortcomings? Make a list of your reasons. Be specific.

_____

_____

_____

2. What defects of character are standing in my way of changing?

_____

_____

_____

Healing Our Brokenness *Psalm 51:16-19*

1. Have the first five steps prepared me to be "entirely ready" for God to work in my heart and my life?

_____

_____

_____

2. In this psalm, David had to grow up a little. He had to accept that he was flawed in God's eyes. He could never bring a sacrifice good or perfect enough to atone for those flaws. Am I still trying to bring God evidence of how good I am, or am I coming to a place of acceptance, as David did? How does acceptance help me to stay in the healing process? Explain.

_____

_____

_____

3. Jesus said, "God blesses those who mourn, for they will be comforted" (Matthew 5:4). In what ways has God comforted me?

_____

_____

_____

God's Abundant Pardon *Isaiah 55:1-9*

1. What ways have I tried to fill the hunger of my soul and the thirst of my spirit with activity, instead of trusting in and following God's will?

_____

_____

_____

2. Do I believe, not just in my head but in my heart, that the life God has for me in the future will be even more satisfying than the one I've lived up to this point? Is my heart willing?

_____

_____

_____

Going Deeper *Jonah 4:4-8*

1. What deeper problems have I uncovered in myself?

_____

_____

_____

2. What difficulties have I suffered that have revealed deeper hurts?

_____

_____

_____

3. Am I willing to have these defects removed by God? Why or why not?

_____

_____

_____

Discovering Hope *John 5:1-15*

When we are ready, God does his part. Our part is to get rid of our excuses, our stubborn resistance, and our fear of change. When we clear out these blocks and become entirely ready, it becomes clear that God must do the rest, because only he can accomplish the miracle of setting our feet on the path of an authentic life again.

1. What are my excuses for not moving forward in my recovery?

_____

_____

_____

2. Have I been stubbornly resistant because I've been afraid of change? Why am I afraid of change?

_____

_____

_____

Attitudes and Actions *Philippians 2:12-14*
This is the attitude of Step Six: "Work hard to show the results of your salvation, obeying God with deep reverence and fear. For God is working in you, giving you the desire and the power to do what pleases him" (Philippians 2:12-13).

1. Do I have a vision for the purposes for which God saved me spiritually? Describe those purposes here.

_____

_____

_____

2. Am I now willing to accept that I will continue taking this step in order to grow, letting go of the old way of life to make room for my new life? Why or why not?

_____

_____

_____

Removing Impatience *James 1:2-4*

1. I am to rejoice, not in the troubles that come my way, but in the opportunities that the troubles present for me to grow. What is my typical attitude toward troubles?

   _____

   _____

   _____

2. How does knowing that my troubles give me the opportunity to grow affect my attitude about my experience of my troubles?

   _____

   _____

   _____

3. How can I develop more patience when troubles come my way?

   _____

   _____

   _____

*First Peter 4:1 tells us to arm ourselves
with the attitude of Christ, who was prepared
and willing to suffer. It's time to get ready.*

STEP 7

PROFILE

Thomas and Sky met at a church camp in Texas where they both became believers and began their spiritual journeys as Christians at the same time. They dated for two years in high school and went to college together. They married the year after they both graduated. They bonded over their musical interests and love of the arts. It was one of many things they shared in common, in addition to their faith. Their early relationship and common values looked like a solid foundation for a bright future together. They wanted to use their musical abilities for the benefit of their church and broader community.

Then, life became complicated. Thomas became sick with a rare blood disorder that sapped him of all of his energy. He was so weak that he could not get out of bed most days. Thomas ran out of sick days quickly, and his boss ran out of patience with him. He soon lost his job. He felt intense shame from losing his job and his health. He began questioning whether God was punishing him or if he simply had bad luck. Depression set in and Thomas's inner rage broke out into fits of anger that included yelling at and threatening Sky. It was so intense that Sky was afraid he might kill himself or her. Sky tried to make peace with Thomas and comply with his wishes. But, secretly, she packed up their two children and moved out of the house in the middle of the night.

Eventually, Sky divorced Thomas, gaining full custody of their two children and ownership of their formerly shared home.

Thomas was left with nothing but a room at the Salvation Army. It was there that he picked up a *Life Recovery Bible* and took his first look at the Twelve Steps. Thomas thought that God did not care about him or did not care enough to help him or fix him. That was how he felt when he read the steps for this first time. But after reading the Twelve Steps fully, he sat down with the chaplain to discuss them. By the time they finished talking, Thomas began to see things from a different perspective.

Thomas began to consider that there really was a God who cares about him. He realized that his current situation stemmed primarily from his reaction to an illness that he could not control. God was always there, but Thomas was either yelling at him, demanding he do something, or ignoring him. He worked through the first five steps quickly but took a while on Step Six. Finally, he asked the God he just barely believed in to remove the problems he was starting to see in himself. That meant the real work had just begun, because asking God to remove his shortcomings required courage to cooperate with God and do the hard work of removal and improvement.

STEP SEVEN
We humbly asked God to remove our shortcomings.

We tend to ask for God's help after every other option has been considered and tried. The longer we delay asking for God to help us, the greater the evidence that we are living in insanity and the longer we prolong our own pain. The good news is that once we have worked Step Six and become entirely ready to have God remove our defects of character, then starting Step Seven is not so difficult.

Step Seven is similar to what we are taught to do if we ever catch on fire: Stop, drop, and roll. Most people remember those three lifesaving words so well that they actually do what they say when they see their clothes on fire. They work here also. To get to Step Seven we have already stopped what we have been doing. We have seen the futility of it, and we have determined it does not work. Secondly, we dropped down to a place of humility. We dropped to a place of humble willingness and became entirely ready to have God remove our defects. Our "roll" is the move to get the job done of letting God transform our character. It is moving out of the dirt and debris of our old lives and moving into a new way of living that brings hope and healing.

Most of us who have been through a divorce have had many occasions when our shortcomings were exposed and explained in great detail. If it was not the person we were married to, then there were family and friends to do the job. Some of us had these shortcomings detailed in court proceedings. The worst pain for many of us was our own rumination over them. We shamed ourselves as we started to see clearly the mistakes we had made and the missteps we had taken. We obsessed over the fact that things we had done could not be undone. We have been tortured with these shortcomings. Finally, we are asking God for help.

Removing our shortcomings requires something beyond just stopping our destructive habits or behaviors. We must not only look at those areas that have hampered our relationship with God, but we must look at how we can open the floodgates of spiritual strength, connection, and insight. These good things come from God, and we need them to transform our shortcomings into strengths. It is a complex process that takes time and attention, but it starts with beginning each day with a request like this:

> God, please help me today to do a little bit better than yesterday. Help me see where I am falling short and how I can relate to you and others differently. Fill me with your spirit today. Help me live spiritually and not just for my own selfish desires. Help me to see others clearly and to respond to them with love and compassion. Amen.

Throughout our lives, our shame has pushed us onto our own self-directed path. We held on to the lie that if the world would just work the way we wanted it to work, and if others would cooperate with us, everything would get better. Now, today and each day forward, we retreat from those old patterns, and we move from trying to control others to reaching for God and requesting his help.

In living out Step Seven, there are some requirements for transformation to occur. Honesty is a must. To simplify it, we need to determine to tell the truth to all others. Recovery through the Twelve Steps is an honesty program, and if we are not committed to it, we are wasting our time. We need to be committed to telling the truth. And when we lie or obscure the truth, we must be committed to quickly admitting it and then telling the truth.

We need to keep in mind that there are different perspectives to truth. There is the truth we know or think we know, but sometimes the way we see things gets distorted. While we want to be faithful to express what we know to be true, we also want to ask God to reveal to us what we might not see. We also want to be open to how others see things, and it might be quite different from our version. Humility speaks the truth we know, seeks to see what we do not know, and wants to understand how others see and experience what is true. If we ask God to make us sensitive to things we do not see, he grants us that. I (Steve) also believe the Holy Spirit will prompt us and make us sensitive to others if we truly desire to relate to others in truth.

God is love. Love is what he does and what he wants from us. It does not always feel like love when we are full of shame or when we are suffering the consequences of our own behavior or when God is disciplining us. But God is love, and we have failed to love him and others. It is the biggest shortcoming we have. So when we ask God to help us, if we are aware of who God is and who we are, we will ask God to help us love better by removing the things preventing us from loving well.

It takes hard work to let God heal us from those past hurts. With God's help, we can see the reality of where we fall short and go to work on it. Gradually we see the sanity emerge because our shortcomings are being replaced with strengths and our will is replaced by daily surrender and cooperation with the God who loves us.

QUESTIONS FOR **STEP SEVEN**

God, My Helper *Exodus 4:1-12*

1. Does the thought of facing life without my spouse frighten me? In what ways?

_____

_____

_____

2. Like Moses, do I make excuses as a way to resist change?

_____

_____

_____

3. How is that part of my unwillingness to let God change me?

_____

_____

_____

Clearing the Mess *Isaiah 57:12-19*

1. Have I developed enough humility from my experiences to see that I need to let God work in my heart? Is there any doubt that my self-reliance has kept God out?

_____

_____

_____

2. Describe the difference between humiliation and humility.

_____

_____

_____

Giving Up Control *Jeremiah 18:1-6*

1. Have I ever demanded that God change circumstances for my benefit? When?

_____

_____

2. Have I ever been impatient about God's timing?

_____

_____

3. What keeps me from letting go so that God can change my life?

_____

_____

4. In my divorce, have I become impatient with God?

_____

_____

Pride Born of Hurt *Luke 11:5-13*

1. Is it hard for me to ask anyone, even God, for help? If yes, why?

_____

_____

_____

2. How has that affected the process of my divorce?

_____

_____

_____

3. What experiences in my family brought about my self-sufficiency?

_____

_____

_____

4. Do I trust God to meet my needs and to walk with me through the next phase of my life? Why or why not?

_____

_____

_____

A Humble Heart *Luke 18:10-14*

1. Have I ever compared my faults, problems, losses, and sins to blatant sins of others in order to avoid deeper work on my own character defects? What does this do for me?

_____

_____

_____

2. While dealing with the issues related to the divorce, have I struggled at all with self-hatred or self-harm? What do I need to do in order to be open with a trusted adviser or counselor about this?

_____

_____

_____

3. Am I humble enough to let others know that I'm willing to face my life as a single person?

_____

_____

_____

An Open Book *Philippians 2:5-9*

1. How important is my image to me?

_____

_____

_____

2. Can I release to God my self-centered fears of being known and of losing my image? Write a prayer to God expressing the desire to do so.

_____

_____

_____

_____

_____

_____

Unending Love *1 John 5:1-15*

1. What blocks me from asking God to do the work of character building and maturation in my heart and life? Describe each block.

_____

_____

_____

2. How confident am I in believing that God is willing to remove my shortcomings? Describe those feelings.

_____

_____

_____

_____

"Shortcomings" is a very polite way of describing sin, weakness, defects in character, addiction, compulsions, dependency—or a thousand other conditions and symptoms that indicate we are falling short of the glory of God and the lives he has called us to live. Asking God to remove our shortcomings is always a joint venture between us and him. Since we have spent much of our lives proving we can't fix ourselves, it is time to finally ask God to do what we will never have the power or insight to do ourselves.

A Prayer for Step Seven

Dear God,
Search my heart and reveal to me any arrogance or pride that is separating me from you, the people around me, and the person you have called me to be. My shortcomings are numerous, and my attempts to fix them always end in failure. Please remove these shortcomings from me. Do for me what I cannot do for myself. Give me the courage to do whatever it takes to become victorious over these problems. Thank you for the work you are doing in me and for the opportunity to transform my life. Amen.

PROFILE

Nancy had the kind of childhood that set the negative trajectory of her relationships for many years to come. Nancy's mother was largely absent from her life. She had a job that paid well, but she had to work long hours that kept her from bonding closely with her family. Nancy's father grew up in an abusive home, and he passed that legacy of abuse on to Nancy. Nancy's father used her as a kind of "surrogate wife" to cope with his absentee spouse. Nancy was the sole focus of her father's attention, which kept her from developing close relationships with her peers. At times, her father became physically and verbally abusive, and then he would act like nothing had happened.

Nancy's experience growing up with the emotional incest of her father on one hand and his fits of rage on the other threw Nancy into a deep sadness that she did not share with anyone. To cope with how she felt she also developed a bad habit: stealing. She wanted something of whatever anyone had. It could be a necklace, a sweater, or a pair of shoes. There was some kind of thrill or satisfaction from this secret sin. She did not examine why she did it, she just took things that were not hers.

When Nancy went to college, she struggled to make friendships last very long. It was difficult for her to connect with other women, but when it came to dating men, she was confident and in control. When she met Clifford her sophomore year, he was a junior and seemed more an equal than any of the other guys she dated. They fell in love and married five days after Nancy graduated.

All of the pain for her began immediately. Every day it seemed like a new disappointment would arise. Everything that she loved about Clifford seemed to die at the wedding. Everything that had once drawn her to him seemed like another excuse to be irritated and angry at him. In her mind, it was all his fault, and so she began to steal from him. Nancy also began to alternately berate and praise him, just like her father had done to her. Clifford did not understand what had caused Nancy to become this way. When Nancy served him with divorce papers, he was neither shocked nor disappointed. He was relieved.

Nancy got everything she wanted in the settlement. She picked up her life and had a few months of celebratory freedom until the misery started to settle in. The desire for the divorce and the immediate relief it brought were replaced by regret, emptiness, and a complete lack of understanding of her life. She called her church and asked if they had a list of Christian counselors in the area. They directed her to a counselor who helped her work through the Twelve Steps of Life Recovery.

The first seven steps presented no problem for Nancy. As she went along, she knew she would have to make confession and restitution eventually, but she blocked it out. It could have been because her counselor was focusing on helping her see some of the wrongs done to her by her father and mother. It had not been easy to understand how her parents' behaviors had hurt her.

Nancy's therapist made sense of her secret compulsion to steal. So much of her childhood had been taken from her that it was not so mysterious that she would be driven to take from others. If there had not been so much trust and respect between Nancy and her therapist, it is unlikely Nancy would have progressed further to do the work required in Steps Eight and Nine. Step Nine seemed like something she would never be able to do, even though she had worked so hard to become entirely ready to cooperate with God. She doubted she would have the courage to do it, but she was willing to do the work of Step Eight because it included becoming willing.

This step was most important in changing Nancy's life. Through making her list of people she had harmed, she was able to see things she had not seen in working Step Four. Now, she stepped out of her denial of her humanity and started to see, accept, and record some mistakes she had made with others, especially Clifford. Seeing the list was painful, but Nancy's life made sense in a whole new and deeper way than ever before.

STEP EIGHT

We made a list of all persons we had harmed and became willing to make amends to them all.

Living one day at a time helps us not get ahead of ourselves. Working the Twelve Steps one step at a time can keep us moving forward, focused on what we need to do without being overwhelmed by the task up ahead. This is especially important in this step. It is also important to stay focused on the first half of this step and only the first half, at first. If you don't, you can become paralyzed thinking how impossible it might be to make amends. Don't skip ahead to Step Nine before you're done working all of Step Eight. For now, let's just focus on that list.

A great place to start is by asking for God's help with making this list of people we have hurt. When we ask God to help us, God can open us up to the truth of our past and help us see and feel in a way we haven't before. We can ask God for new insight on all that we have done and the impact that it has had on others. Sometimes we struggle to see our innate value or realize all the positive influences we have had on others. This step can be tough because it is focused on the harm that we have done. If it pushes you down into a deeper depression, or you feel so bad that you don't want to continue, you are not alone. Now is the time to reach out to a counselor or find a sponsor who has experienced this before you. Things that feel impossible alone are quite doable with someone else.

When we start making our lists, sometimes little voices become big roadblocks. They tell us that we don't really need to do this. They tell us that we have grown past this point in life. Whatever those little voices tell you, tell them to be quiet long enough for you to hear God's much bigger voice. God's voice says this in Luke 6:31, "Do to others as you would like them to do to you." It's the standard for loving others the way God wants us to. We feel good when others treat us this way, so people will appreciate it when we do the same. This perspective is intended to get us thinking about who needs to be on the list. It's important for us to think about other people, but in the end, we are the ones who benefit far beyond anyone on our list from this step.

When we make something right with someone else, we are making it right with God. Jesus taught us that when we come to worship him, and we remember that we have offended some-one, we must go and make amends first (Matthew 5:23-24). Making things right with others benefits our relationship with God. When we make things right with others, it also benefits us more than we probably can imagine until we do it. If we don't make it right with others, we live with the guilt and shame and self-loathing that we feel from doing something harmful to someone else. When we are not dealing with what is not right, our anxiety over it leads to destructive behaviors and unhealthy distractions. Once we pay what we owe, we free ourselves from the shameful obsession that has stopped us from living the life of freedom God wants for us.

We don't have to worry about the cost of restitution or how we are going to do it just yet. All we have to do at this stage is to write our list. If we have stolen money from someone, it is obvious that they go on the list. There are others that might not be so obvious. Harm can come in the form of remaining silent when it would have helped someone to speak up. We might have adult children who are still upset with us because they know we could have said something or done something to help them but instead enabled or allowed abuse to continue. Silence is just one form of betrayal or abandonment.

The second half of this step focuses on doing what it takes to become willing to make amends to all the people we have harmed. It seems we would not struggle with this if we did the work needed to become entirely ready to cooperate with God, but recovery is an evolving process. Some of us have to become entirely ready all over again to be willing to make amends to everyone on the list. To be ready, we have to remind ourselves that we do not have what it takes on our own to turn things around. So, in humility, we recognized that God has done it before for others, and God will do it for us. We asked for God's help knowing that God is love, but God is also tough. Making amends is tough, but it is the loving thing to do. Loving and doing hard things is consistent with God. He doesn't want us to make amends in order to punish or shame us. He wants us to make amends because of the benefit involved.

Making amends with others also restores intimacy with God. God loves you and wants a relationship with you. Making amends lowers your anxiety and allows you to be more at ease in every situation. The burden of shame is lifted. The fear of being found out is no more. You might even have your first experience of serenity in the midst of conflict and turmoil. And the downside? None. Because even the discomfort you experience now makes you stronger in the long term.

Three things can help in developing the willingness to do this difficult task. Humility teaches us to be aware and admit we need God's help, no matter what path God takes us down. Support from others will encourage us and help us have courage in the toughest moments. Clarity of mind helps us to see the remarkable benefit of freedom from the past, redemptive connection in the present, and hope for the future.

QUESTIONS FOR **STEP EIGHT**

Making Restitution *Exodus 22:10-15*

1. How have I failed to respect the property of others?

_____

_____

_____

2. How have I avoided responsibility?

_____

_____

_____

3. What excuses have I used for not looking at my own behaviors?

_____

_____

_____

Unintentional Sins *Leviticus 4:1-28*

1. In what ways have I unintentionally harmed others with my words, moods, self-pity, depression, anger, or fears?

_____

_____

_____

2. In what ways have I acted thoughtlessly without regard for others' needs or feelings?

_____

_____

_____

Scapegoats *Leviticus 16:20-22*

1. Have I been putting off making a list because I am afraid of some responses? Who am I afraid of? Why?

_____

_____

_____

2. Is there someone I'm having trouble forgiving who blocks my willingness to work through this step? Who?

_____

_____

_____

Coming out of Isolation *Ecclesiastes 4:9-12*

1. How have I allowed isolation to block or slow down my facing the reality of my divorce?

_____

_____

_____

2. What is the role of shame and guilt in my isolation?

_____

_____

_____

3. Am I willing to forgive myself for the hurt I've caused others? How about forgiving myself for the hurt I have caused myself? Write a prayer of willingness to forgive.

_____

_____

_____

Forgiving Others, Forgiving Yourself *Matthew 18:23-35*

1. Are there people on my list that I am having trouble forgiving for their part in our relationship? Who and why?

_____

_____

_____

2. What stops me from letting others off the hook? Fear? Resentment? Care taking?

_____

_____

_____

3. What blocks me from forgiving others for the wrongs they have done to me?

   a. Fear of what others would think of me?
   b. Fear of letting others see my hurts?
   c. Fear of conflict?
   d. Protecting others' feelings to avoid conflict?

_____

_____

_____

Grace-Filled Living *2 Corinthians 2:5-8*

1. Is there anyone, either on my list or not, whose behaviors I do not approve of? Who? Why?

_____

_____

_____

2. Am I willing to let go of judgment and disapproval to open myself up to the recovery process and to working this step?

_____

_____

_____

3. Have I been so afraid of rejection that I have delayed my recovery process? What about my willingness to make amends?

_____

_____

_____

The Power of Words *James 3:5-10*

1. Words can hurt terribly. Who has been hurt by my misuse of words?

_____

_____

_____

2. James calls the tongue a "flame of fire." How have I tamed my tongue?

_____

_____

_____

3. What have been the consequences of my misuse of words?

_____

_____

_____

Remember, it's about willingness!

9

PROFILE

Nancy, whom we met in Step Eight, completed her list, and with her therapist, worked through her points of resistance until she became willing to make amends. Her willingness was not that difficult to develop in the end. First, she admitted that she would want someone to make amends with her if that person had harmed her in any way. Second, she saw what life had become for her while carrying around all the unresolved wrongs she had committed against God and others. She knew she needed to make things right on all fronts. Third, she believed it would introduce her to a freedom she had not experienced as an adult. She wanted what others had said they experienced after they had cleared their consciences by making amends. Fourth, it was the next right thing to do—it was the right, moral, honest, and responsible thing to do.

She began her list with people she had stolen from. If it was a store, she calculated how much she had taken plus interest, and sent cash with a letter of apology, anonymously. The more difficult payments were for people she knew and had stolen from. She humbled herself, met with those she could, and returned to them what she owed. She apologized and asked for them to forgive her, and in every case they welcomed her apology and act of making amends. She also met with and apologized to people she had prematurely ended friendships with and anyone she had lied to or spread rumors about. Through phone calls, e-mails, in-person meetings, or letters, she contacted them all, and everyone welcomed her apologies.

The toughest person on the list was Clifford. They met for dinner, and Nancy shared with him the work she had been doing with her therapist and the Twelve Steps. She told him that she saw what she had done to him. She detailed times when she had been critical of everything he did and cruel in her rejection of him. She asked him to forgive her, and he said he already had done so. Over dinner Clifford told her he had forgiven her because he had wanted to get on with his life. He believed Nancy was sincere and hoped the best for her. There were many tears during that dinner, but by the time dessert came, there were many smiles and even some laughter.

In the years to come, if someone asked Nancy what her favorite color is, she would say white. While not actually a color, it was the feeling she carried within her. Making amends had wiped her slate clean, and she felt white as snow rather than the deep darkness of shame. When asked if she had a favorite number, she would say eight and nine because it was the combination of those two steps that had the most profound impact on her life. Finally, when asked how she liked to spend her time away from work, she would reply, "Living life free of shame." Not a bad way to live.

STEP NINE

We made direct amends to such people wherever possible, except when to do so would injure them or others.

Making direct amends puts actions to the emotions we feel and the words we have painfully written. It is the culmination of awareness of how we have hurt someone, along with the willingness to make it right. It finally brings us to the place where we must act on what we know to be true. We have searched our past and our hearts and know we have hurt some people. We have listed how we have hurt them, and we know what we need to do. For some it is a letter we need to write. For others a face-to-face meeting is appropriate. For others it is a phone call. In rare instances it might be an e-mail due to the offended person being in some obscure location. And still, for others, there is monetary compensation to be made. When we are fully willing, we are as compelled to make it right as we were compelled to do whatever we did to hurt them. At some point, we say to ourselves, "Let the amends begin."

There has never been a time when it has been easier to locate people and make it right with them. Various social media platforms and online search tools put most everyone within reach. When we become willing to make amends, it is often shocking to us how people show back up in our lives or how we find them. No matter how we find them or where we find them, each person needs to be considered individually so that the way we make amends is the most appropriate.

If we are like most people, admitting we were wrong and asking for forgiveness is what needs to be done in most cases. For those who are closest to us, a meeting will be more appropriate than a phone call or a letter. For some it will be a short meal or a cup of coffee, but for many more it will be a simple conversation after church or work or wherever we think appropriate. It is a time to tell the person we have been thinking about them, we are aware of the hurtful things we did, and we are asking them to forgive us for those things. We do it with sincerity and care for the other person, and we realize they may not be ready to forgive us. As much as it was up to us, we did what we could do to make amends.

Phone calls and letters can be just as simple. Phone calls can be the best way to handle most situations because they are less threatening and the stakes feel lower for the other person. For others a letter will mean a lot. Getting a handwritten letter shows we cared enough to do something out of the ordinary. It also gives the other person space and time to respond in the way that is most comfortable for them. We would not want to indicate that we expect a response or demand one, but we do want to make it easy for them to phone, write, or e-mail if they want to do so.

There are other types of amends that require more than words. If you stole money, figure out a way to pay it back. If you can't cover the amount with a check at the time you contact the person, tell them how you plan to pay them back in installments. If you are at a place where there is no way to come up with any money, then be humble and offer to do some work for them to show that you are sincere in your desire to make things right.

When someone was betrayed in a marriage, security, dreams, trust, and peace were all stolen from the partner. When the confession is over, there have been several cases where all of the assets from the marriage settlement were turned over to the betrayed spouse. It is extreme, but it is a solid step toward healing the relationship. If you do not know what to do, ask the person you hurt what they think might make things right, and if you are able to do it, make amends the way they desire.

The second aspect of this step—when making amends would injure the other party—is tricky. It can be used as an excuse not to do what needs to be done. We can make assumptions about the responses or reactions of others that let us off the hook. Our default could be to assume it would hurt the person or do more damage than good. That, of course, is not the purpose of this qualifier. The purpose of it is to protect people whose lives have gone on since being hurt by us. We believe those times are much fewer than most people believe, and there are other ways to handle amends and restitution than just to assume it would be best not to contact the person.

The qualifier mentions that if it might cause problems for others, it would be best to not make direct contact. Included in the word *others* could be you. If you have been involved in an affair, the last thing you want to do is to have any interaction with that person. You must protect the other person and yourself from stirring up whatever it was that led to the affair. Avoid that kind of contact and any other that would cause harm to you and those who love you.

That brings us to what is called the "living amends." If it would cause damage to contact the person or the person has died, then the living amends is a tool that makes things right within us. To make it right, we make sacrifices for or serve in some way someone other than the person we hurt. We grow and get help and allow the mistake we made to be the first step toward growing and maturing. We let our character growth be evidence that the pain we caused someone else was the catalyst for learning, growing, and becoming the person God called us to be. When we look back on the hurt we caused, we are able to remember the work we did and the contributions we made to others in an attempt to make it right without causing any more damage.

QUESTIONS FOR STEP NINE

A Feared Encounter *Genesis 33:1-11*

1. Who are the people on my Step Eight list who strike the most intense fear in my heart when I think about making amends face-to-face?

_____

_____

_____

2. Do I have support people who will remind me again of my willingness to take such a challenging step?

_____

_____

_____

Keeping Promises *2 Samuel 9:1-9*

1. How has my divorce made me aware of people with whom I need to make amends?

_____

_____

_____

2. Is there anyone to whom I owe amends due to forgetting to fulfill a promise?

_____

_____

_____

Hope for Those Making Amends *Ezekiel 33:10-16*

1. What type of amends listed in Step Eight do I resist? Why?

_____

_____

_____

2. What are the fears that are keeping me from the life-giving process of Step Nine?

_____

_____

_____

Peacemaking *Matthew 5:23-26*

1. Am I a peacekeeper or peacemaker?

_____

_____

_____

2. What is my usual response or reaction to brokenness?

_____

_____

_____

3. Does my amends list include people who have something against me? Does that make it hard for me to have the courage to deal with them?

_____

_____

_____

The Blessing of Giving _Luke 19:1-10_

1. List the financial amends that you owe. Name the people and amounts.

_____

_____

_____

2. Am I willing to go to any length to offer amends, even if it calls for payments?

_____

_____

_____

A Clean Slate _Ephesians 2:8-10_

1. How does knowing I've been saved by grace, that my heart is clean before God, help me make amends with people?

_____

_____

_____

2. What did I learn from this passage about being made clean, being shaped into God's masterpiece?

_____

_____

_____

3. What does my making amends say about my character?

_____

_____

_____

Unfinished Business _Philemon 1:13-16_

1. Have any relationships or past wrongs come to light in the process of recovery where I still need to make amends?

_____

_____

_____

2. Do I have any unfinished business left on my list?

_____

_____

_____

3. Am I waiting for the certainty of forgiveness before I make amends? Why am I afraid of a lack of certainty?

_____

_____

_____

A Servant's Heart *1 Peter 2:18-25*

1. Am I reluctant to make amends while I am dealing with my divorce?

_____

_____

_____

2. Do I fear that painful consequences will cause me more suffering? If so, what is the worst that could happen?

_____

_____

_____

3. Which of the previous steps do I need to focus on before making these fearsome amends?

_____

_____

_____

4. Do I trust God's will for me if I follow the challenge of Step Nine?

_____

_____

_____

> *There is a price to be paid for freedom,*
> *and it is called restitution.*

PROFILE

Reba and Andy lived in Delaware where they had a very successful life together. Years before, they had taken over her family's four hardware stores. Andy was great with people and numbers, and after ten years of growing those businesses, they received an offer to sell that they could not refuse.

Reba and Andy were instantly thrust into a level of wealth that brought them freedom from the pressures most people faced, but they suddenly had a whole lot of time with each other that caused more problems than either imagined. Andy was bored, and after six months of a lot of golf, poker, beer, and television, he was miserable and completely disconnected from Reba. They parented pretty well together, but they could not keep their misery from the kids. After about a year of this new way of living, the summer home in Florida became a fall, winter, and spring retreat for both of them—separately.

Reba and Andy began spending time separately at their vacation home ten days at a time. The plan was to give each other the time and space they needed to recharge individually. Reba was hopeful that would allow them to come back and reconnect in a healthy way. Reba was able to fake it pretty well in front of the kids, but she was sinking deeper and deeper into depression and despair.

When she made her first trek down to the summer home, she was restless. So she went to a local restaurant by herself and ate at the bar. It was there that she struck up a conversation with another woman who was alone. The other woman seemed like a long-lost best friend, and after dinner Reba invited her over to her house where they talked long into the night. The two of them got together the next day, and after hearing about Reba's depression and despair, her new friend offered her something that promised to provide relief. The friend pulled a small bag of pills from her purse, took one, and offered one to Reba, telling her it was meth. Reba, on her own and accountable to no one, quickly said yes and took it. Fifteen minutes later, she was euphoric and felt like she could conquer the world.

That was the beginning of her relationship with methamphetamines. Her addiction very quickly progressed from taking pills to smoking and snorting this highly addictive drug. She phoned Andy and told him she was going to stay another five days. On the fourteenth day of her trip, Reba was in a bar laughing and drinking with another woman, who just happened to be an undercover cop. When Reba was asked, she offered to share some of the twenty grams of powder she had just purchased. She was arrested for possessing more than fourteen grams of methamphetamine, which is a third-degree felony punishable by up to five years in prison and a fine of up to five thousand dollars.

The next phone call Andy received from Reba was not what he expected. Andy took advantage of the arrest, and soon after he filed for divorce and full custody of the kids. Within a year he got everything he wanted, and Reba went to prison to carry out her six-month sentence.

For Reba, this was the beginning of her recovery. She joined a Life Recovery group in prison and started working the steps. The steps worked for her depression. They also helped her kick her quickly developed addiction to meth. And they helped her work through the loss of her marriage and custody of her children. In prison, they gave her a *Life Recovery Bible*, and by the end of her time there, she had worked through all Twelve Steps.

Eventually, she called to make amends with Andy and asked him to forgive her for the criticism, blame, judgment, and manipulation she had thrown his way. She also asked him to forgive her for being irresponsible with their money, their reputation, and her parenting of the kids. She saw it from his perspective, and he was quite moved. But for Andy, it was difficult at first to know what was real and what was a result of her wanting out of prison as soon as possible and needing his support.

But it was real, and as Andy and the children interacted with her more, Andy saw that it was real. He did not know it, but Reba was committed to Step Ten above and beyond any other step or principle. She was committed to living the Twelve Steps every day of her life. The changes in Reba were remarkable to her family.

When she was discharged from prison, she moved back to be near her kids. Rather than hide in shame she went to recovery meetings at church and was involved with the kids' schools. Andy could not believe it. He was fascinated at first. Then his respect for her was at an all-time high and so were his positive feelings. Once Reba was six months out of prison, Andy asked her on a date. She accepted. Six months later they were remarried and began to live one of the greatest redemptive divorce stories ever. The Twelve Steps provided the foundation of their story, but Step Ten was vitally important to their reunion. She never stopped taking that personal inventory, and when she was wrong, she promptly admitted it.

STEP TEN

We continued to take personal inventory, and when we were wrong, promptly admitted it.

You might call Step Ten the step of all steps. It is the one step that involves accepting that recovery cannot be done alone. It is done by being humble under the guidance of a power greater than ourselves—God. It requires that we continue to take an insightful inside look at ourselves. We need to inventory the good, the bad, and the ugly. We don't obsess over the good things, but we are glad they are there. We recognize that we have defects, but we make confession when we are wrong. Beyond that we make amends on an ongoing basis. We do it willingly every day, and as a result we grow closer to God and closer to the ones we love.

When we continue to take a personal inventory, we are mindful of the moment and what we are doing in it. We are living in the present and aware of our own actions and the impact those actions have on others. Our goal is to live a reflective life. We take the time to look back and review the day. When we see where we have fallen short, we don't waste time before owning up to it and making things right with anyone who has been hurt. It is an effective way to live and move forward without carrying damaging shame along with us.

For so much of our lives, we have tried to be in control and manage the outcome of our lives. As our marriages started to unravel, many of us felt like we could manipulate or create an outcome that would be to our liking. When we are trying to manage and control things, we are acting totally independent from God. We become our own higher power. As we practice Step Ten well, we learn to totally depend on God. We can depend on his love and care so that we can take a risk and live free.

The word "promptly" cannot be ignored in this step. If we put off doing what we know we need to do, there is a chance we will never get back to doing what needs to be done. It has never been easier than it is today to quickly move on to another distraction and miss the moment for relational repair and restoration. We need to always act promptly as we continue to walk in peace and serenity. And the sooner we make it right, the sooner the other person doesn't have to grapple with whatever pain or discomfort we have caused. This call to prompt action keeps us current and prevents us from building up shame and regret.

The following verse is a caution to anyone and everyone who is recovering from anything: "If you think you are standing strong, be careful not to fall" (1 Corinthians 10:12). Step Ten is an effective way to make sure this does not happen. For one thing, standing strong feels much different than being humble, taking inventory, and then admitting we have made a mistake. Continuing to work Step Ten is a way of being careful not to fall or relapse.

Relapse has always been a process that starts with complacency. Complacency leads to confusion about whether or not we even have a problem or how severe our problem was or whether or not we even need to be recovering. From there, we are destined to get into some kind of trouble, such as a relationship that starts too soon or would have been better not to start at all. Step Ten keeps us from complacency and not moving forward.

There are some indicators that we are actively carrying out Step Ten. If we are, we will have recently spoken some of the following phrases:

"I am so sorry."

"I regret how I handled that."

"I was wrong."

"I want to ask for your forgiveness."

"I need to make something right with you."

If these kinds of phrases are not coming from us, there is a good chance we are not humbling ourselves to promptly admit our wrongs. Or it could be that we are too busy to stop, reflect, and take an ongoing inventory. If we are too busy, our serenity has been lost and we need to notice that by taking an inventory of what is right about our lives and what needs to be made right. It can be difficult from time to time to live like this, but the difficulty we endure is worth it because it keeps us on a solid path of recovery with redemptive relationships and with the Redeemer of all of our pain.

QUESTIONS FOR **STEP TEN**

Setting Personal Boundaries *Genesis 31:45-55*

1. In order to restore trust in some of my relationships, what particular weaknesses do I need to set boundaries around?

_____

_____

_____

2. Is there a trusted person to whom I can clearly define my commitments? Who? What commitments am I willing to make?

_____

_____

_____

Weeding the Garden *Matthew 13:1-23*

1. While growing in my recovery, some weeds will crop up in my life. How can I do a daily personal inventory to keep the weeds in check?

_____

_____

_____

2. What are some of the "weeds" in my life?

_____

_____

_____

3. How big are my issues, or "weeds"? (Maybe that's why I need a big God!)

_____

_____

_____

Repeated Forgiveness _Romans 5:3-5_

1. Do certain behaviors and character defects that show up in my Step Ten inventory point to a pattern? Which ones? What is being revealed?

_____

_____

_____

2. Am I having trouble admitting these properly in forgiving myself?

_____

_____

_____

3. Do I give myself grace? Why or why not?

_____

_____

_____

Be Angry and Don't Sin _Ephesians 4:26-27_

1. How have I experienced anger in my recovery?

_____

_____

_____

2. What is my first response when I am angry?

_____

_____

_____

3. How was anger dealt with in my family? By my mother? By my father? Which pattern do I follow?

_____

_____

_____

4. When I am angry, can I promptly admit it? Why or why not?

_____

_____

_____

5. Do I have support people who can help me learn to deal with anger more appropriately? Do I have someone I can talk with about my anger? Am I willing to ask for help?

_____

_____

_____

Spiritually Fit _1 Timothy 4:7-8_

1. Since this continual inventory is important for spiritual fitness, where in my daily routine can I set aside time to make self-assessment part of every day?

_____

_____

_____

2. Do I have any resistance to evaluating my defects daily? What are my objections?

_____

_____

_____

_____

3. Here's an example of a simple, daily personal inventory:

   Where have I been selfish, dishonest, fearful, or inconsiderate?

   What have I done right today?

   What do I need God's help with tomorrow?

   What am I grateful for today?

   _____

   _____

   _____

   _____

   _____

Looking in the Mirror *James 1:21-25*

1. Have I been quick to recognize but not to take action in a particular area of my life, or do I ignore a defect of character? If so, can I take action without self-criticism by going back through Steps Six through Nine to work on that particular area or defect?

   _____

   _____

   _____

2. In what area or about what defect do I need to take action today? This week? This month?

_____

_____

_____

Recurrent Sins *1 John 1:8-10*

1. Have I hoped for immediate release from my defects? Have I personally or unknowingly hoped that by doing all the step work I could attain perfection? Write any thoughts and feelings that arise from reading this meditation.

_____

_____

_____

2. Is it clear that I still need inventories to continue my spiritual growth? Explain.

_____

_____

_____

3. Do I sense that my conscience is returning or developing so that I may always more easily recognize my faults? Am I humble enough to admit that more readily? Record any progress.

_____

_____

_____

Our lives require an ongoing evaluation
of our thoughts, deeds, desires, and motives.

PROFILE

Ben was a doer, and Jamie was a feeler. They did not realize how different they were until after their wedding. They had not known each other very long before getting engaged, and the engagement was short. Once Ben decided he was going to do something, he got on with doing it. They were sexually active from the beginning, so the emotional side of the relationship was neglected. It was all romance and intensity, and in that, they missed who they were. On the honeymoon, their differences started to emerge.

On a beach in the Bahamas, Jamie was ready to just sit in the sand, soak up the sun, and recover from a bigger-than-life wedding. But Ben was ready for their first adventures together. He had several adventurous activities planned that day and each day that followed during their honeymoon. The adventures included kayaking, snorkeling, jet skiing, diving with sharks, a deep-sea fishing trip, and a four-wheeler experience. He had all of the activities packed into their seven-day honeymoon, but she was ready to pack it all up and go back home after the third day. Going all the time was not her idea of a honeymoon.

It actually was the beginning of the end. In less than a year, Jamie moved out, and within two years, their divorce was final. Jamie had no tolerance for Ben's lack of awareness of who she was and what she needed. Pleading, discussing, and threatening had not gotten his attention. Ben thought he made a horrible mistake, and the sooner he was out of it the better.

Once the divorce was final, misery, regret, and shame set in. Jamie had not been the problem, and Ben was starting to sense that he had one. At his work, there was a guy who had continued to ask him if he would go to church with him. Finally, Ben agreed to go, rather than be alone for another Sunday. When he went, he didn't fully understand everything the pastor preached about, but by the time it was over, Ben's heart was open in a way it had never been before. The following week he attended his first meeting that would help him work the Twelve Steps so he could recover from his divorce. It would also help him uncover the spiritual man that had been there within him but ignored for too long.

Ben attended the group regularly and made the most of his time there. He started working the steps and growing through each one. It was quite a transformation that grew deeper and deeper as Ben went from being a doer to becoming a relater and a connector, too. When Ben reached Step Eleven he was all in and ready to experience what that step had for him. And because Step Eleven was not a one-time event, Ben entered into a spiritual intimacy with God that brought him meaning, purpose, and a life full of love and serenity. Why? Because Ben never stopped living out all that he found in Step Eleven.

STEP ELEVEN

We sought through prayer and meditation to improve our conscious contact with God, praying only for knowledge of his will for us and the power to carry it out.

We could make the case that real living begins and is sustained by living out Step Eleven. No matter what we have been through or the pain we have suffered, Step Eleven makes everyone equal or, more accurately, elevates us all. When we live out Step Eleven, we are able to live deeply connected to God. Serenity, peace, and security fill us as we have more of God and less of the world and all of its fading glories.

Prayer is not something we only do in the morning or at night or before meals. It becomes a way of life. We read in Colossians 4:2: "Devote yourselves to prayer with an alert mind and a thankful heart." Our self-talk is replaced by praying without ceasing. We don't mumble or complain under our breath, but we carry on a conversation with God. We thank him for all that blesses us, and we ask him to help us with the things and people that do not. Our lives are spiritually focused, so we naturally build and grow our relationship with God through prayer that grows deeper and richer over time. We are reminded of how much time Christ spent in prayer with God, and we emulate that practice. As we live this way, the weight of the world becomes much lighter and much more manageable. We can also meditate on Scripture and hear God's voice in his Word.

Spending time with God and meditating on God's truth results in us becoming aware of what God wants for all people and especially aware of his will for us individually. We are not motivated by the standards of this world. The drive for instant gratification and quick relief is replaced with this need to know God deeply and the desire to spend time with God. Fulfillment and meaning eradicate any need for instant relief or a cheap high. What a joy to have worked the steps and worked through all of the triggers, conflicts, and wounds that have held sway over our mood swings. When we are at peace with God, we have no need to alter our moods and we have the strength to stave off despair or hopelessness.

We also have new strength that is available to us. We can confidently ask God for the strength and power to do what we have come to know is his will for us. There in those old ways of living, we believed our shameful ways disqualified us from knowing God's will or having the strength or power to carry it out. Now we are living a dream of life beyond a regretful past and above any constraining circumstances. We are happier, healthier, and more hopeful than ever because we know we have a relationship with God, who will help us get where we're trying to go.

Knowing God's will can be seen on two levels. First, there are some things that God always wants us to do. God wants us to be humble. We know that arrogance destroys our relationship with God. We also know that God wants us to do the "next right thing." So when given a choice, we know the right choice, which is often the toughest choice, and we make that choice rather than an easier but inappropriate choice. In addition to these choices, we also come to sense a greater calling to serve God. As we intimately connect with God, a sense of a path or picture of a future starts to form.

Caught up in this type of living, we learn to "wait upon the LORD" (Isaiah 40:31, KJV) rather than act impulsively. As we wait for God's timing, we are not anxious, because we have become utterly dependent on God. We persevere through challenges that come up, rather than retreat from them. In fact, we don't panic, and we ask God to use these adversities to grow us up in godly character and to bring us closer to him.

We know of no one who sets out to experience a divorce. We can see it coming, be blind to the possibility, or can initiate it, but it is never plan A. For some it provides relief from a relationship with someone who has consistently misled, mistreated, and betrayed them. For others, it is the shattering of a dream or the evidence that the dream has been shattered for a very long time. For almost everyone it is painful beyond what anyone expected. Loss is compounded upon loss, and for most, despair and hopelessness make every day a struggle to survive or just get through it all.

Working the Twelve Steps counters all of this. Step by step, we deal with the reality before us. We come to see our irresponsible actions and shortcomings and contributions to the demise of the relationship. We do what we can to make things right even in instances where we may not be entirely at fault. It does not matter because we are just focused on what we need to do. As we continue to work the steps we eventually land on Step Eleven. We need Step Eleven because it helps us live well, in spite of all we see around us. It is a key to recovery and restoration for each of us as wonderfully created and loved creatures of God. As we live according to this powerful step, we come to realize that even when the worst things imaginable happen, God uses them to transform us. Eventually, we are able to look back and see that what we thought was the end of our lives was in fact a new beginning.

QUESTIONS FOR STEP ELEVEN

God Is for Me *Job 19:8-27*

1. In my working the steps, has God felt like my enemy? In what ways?

_____

_____

_____

2. Am I tempted to do God's will in my own power? In what situations?

_____

_____

_____

Thirst for God *Psalm 27:1-6*

1. What am I seeking most from God?

_____

_____

_____

2. What is most difficult about trusting God with my requests?

_____

_____

_____

Joy in God's Presence _Psalm 65:1-4_

1. What keeps me from accepting and experiencing God's comfort?

_____

_____

_____

2. What scares me about the probability that God wants to redeem my divorce in some way?

_____

_____

_____

Finding God _Psalm 105:1-9_

1. Am I changing from day to day? Am I moving through the process? Identify some ways that things are changing.

_____

_____

_____

2. Am I becoming more aware of others' feelings and needs? What have I noticed today?

_____

_____

_____

3. Make a list of things you can thank God for today.

_____

_____

_____

Powerful Secrets *Psalm 119:1-11; Luke 2:16-20*

1. What Scriptures have I hidden in my heart in the midst of my recovery?

_____

_____

_____

2. Meditation means to ponder Scripture throughout the day. What has been easy about meditation? What has been difficult?

_____

_____

_____

3. Has meditation helped me? How?

_____

_____

_____

Patient Waiting *Isaiah 40:28-31*

1. How does impatience show itself in my recovery? In my relationship with God?

_____

_____

_____

2. Am I impatient about my progress in recovery? Do I expect perfection?

_____

_____

_____

3. Why is it hard for me to trust in the Lord?

_____

_____

_____

Enjoying the Calm _Matthew 16:24-26; Galatians 6:9_

1. In what ways am I addicted to chaos?

_____

_____

_____

2. Why has chaos felt more comfortable for me than the calm of recovery?

_____

_____

_____

3. How does focusing on doing God's will introduce me to the calm?

_____

_____

_____

God is on our side,
even if we can't see it now.

PROFILE

Jacob was a brilliant man who had Asperger's syndrome, which means that he was highly capable of focusing on his work but less capable of reading social cues and emotions. His brilliance allowed him to see problems and their potential solutions from a perspective others could not. It was quite phenomenal that he could be so intelligent and creative with facts and figures, but when it came to people, such as his wife, Marla, he had no clue how to connect meaningfully for an extended length of time. He could implement new behaviors and carry them out for a while, but within a few days he would drift back into his old way of relating.

Like many others with Asperger's, Jacob could not read faces and discern emotional states. He could not tell the difference between someone who was irritated and someone who was afraid because they just saw a mouse in the kitchen. Emotions are not facts. The emotions others felt did not register in his brain the way that data did. For Marla, it felt like being married to a man who intellectually understood the concept of love and thought he loved but was not engaged in the process of a loving and nurturing relationship. She tried pleasing him in every way possible. Great trips for just the two of them did nothing to change anything when they returned home. Perhaps she could have adjusted if he had stayed at his ongoing level of disconnection, but he did not. One day, he had an idea for a concentrated packet of nutrition that would quickly replenish the body of someone who was starving. It was cheap, easy to ship by the ton, and would prevent thousands of deaths. It would be his most significant contribution to the world.

Jacob became obsessed with his lifesaving invention. He had to figure out every detail from perfecting the formula to packaging, shipping, and distribution. He thought Marla would understand why he was driven to create an answer to world hunger crises. He assumed she was as excited about the prospect as he was, but she was not. Marla wanted a life alongside whatever he was doing. She went from wanting to please him to wanting to push him out of the car onto the pavement. Marla's anger and rage intensified, which motivated Jacob to keep his distance. With no heart-to-heart connection, she rented a studio apartment, furnished it, and handed him the keys to go and live in it away from her.

The moment Jacob walked out the door to live away from her, Marla felt relief. It was not long before she took the next step and filed for divorce. He thought it was a game she was playing to get him to change. But it was not a game, and the judge declaring that their marriage had been terminated was proof. Through the divorce, his work was interrupted with depositions and legal counsel and court appearances. He could see why she would not want to be married to him, and he complied with what the judge and his attorney required of him. When it was final, he actually felt relief because he would no longer be interrupted with the demands that the divorce process made on him.

Jacob's misery set in about a year after the divorce. It took him that long to look up from his work and realize what a horrible life he was living. It was at that exact time that he met a man at Cracker Barrel, where he ate most of his breakfasts. This man was usually there talking with one or two other men over breakfast. One day he approached Jacob and struck up a conversation. That conversation led to many more that developed into Wednesday morning breakfasts together. After a few weeks this man became very aware of Jacob's misery. At the right time the man invited Jacob to join him at the church a couple of blocks from Cracker Barrel at a recovery meeting for men going through a divorce or dealing with the aftermath of a divorce. It was uncomfortable for Jacob to be there, but he stuck it out, and one year later he had worked through the Twelve Steps and walked into a new way of living.

The Twelve Steps did not cure Jacob of Asperger's or make the symptoms of it go away. But they helped him make things right with those who had been hurt by him. The steps helped him stay current, and they gave him a new mission in life. Attending the group gave him a connection with others who were on his team. They did not judge him. They loved him and cared about him, and soon he was committed to helping others through that group. Jacob would tell anyone he met about the group and encourage them to tell anyone who had been through a divorce to give it a try. The group grew due to his one-man marketing campaign! Jacob found a new mission in life through that group. He started going early to make coffee and set up chairs. Eventually, he became one of the group facilitators. The group became his way of carrying the message to others. He had known misery, and he wanted to help others avoid it or get out of it.

For a man who had great difficulty with relationships, it was surprising how much Jacob enjoyed talking to people who came to the group. He learned to ask some deeper questions, and he learned to listen and respond to the answers. It became his lifeline out of the disconnection caused by his Asperger's. After a year of being with the group he was fully engaged, and he surrendered one last thing that needed to go. He gave up trying to figure out how to improve on the Twelve Steps. With a smile on his face, he looked up at the stars and said to God, "Okay." And with that he continued to work the steps without trying to revise them. He was fully committed to grow with them and carry the message of hope, help, and healing to others who needed to heal from divorce.

STEP TWELVE

Having had a spiritual awakening as a result of these steps, we tried to carry this message to others, and to practice these principles in all our affairs.

This wonderful twelfth step is often treated as an appendix or an add-on to the program. It gets minimized into simply helping others. Helping others is very important and incredibly valuable, but this step is so much more than that. The first part gives us a reason to do what the last two parts of the step tell us to do, or more accurately, what Bill Wilson is telling us he did—what they all did—to get and stay sober. When we work the steps, by the time we get to Step Twelve, we have had a spiritual awakening. It begins with Step One, where we acknowledge that all of the nonspiritual effort put forth by us under our own power is not enough for us to manage our lives.

That is the beginning of our wake-up call. When we wake up to our limitations, we begin a spiritual awakening. Then we can begin the process of turning our unmanageable lives over to God and working with God, rather than against God, to recover from our problems. Some of us caused the divorce because we did not want to live amid pain and betrayal anymore. Others of us did not cause it, but our reactions are just as earth-oriented as our spouse's. We enter into the steps because we discovered that they are a different way of seeing the world and living in it. It is a spiritual path, and it awakens us to a different kind of life.

Having had a spiritual awakening means that we are awakened to truth. It is God's truth. His truth tells us that we are not alone, that he is with us. It tells us that we do not have to live in shame because when we come to him, he forgives us and sets us on a path not just of recovery but of restoration. In other words, when you have surgery and recover, you are able to walk out of the hospital. Restoration postsurgery means we regain our original strength from before the problem that caused us to need surgery. In our restoration, we recover from the devastation of divorce, then we restore the broken relationship we recognize along the way. We start with God. But it is more than that. Our spiritual awakening leads us to a place known as "weller than well." We walk a spiritual path that we have never walked before, and over time we are not just back to where we were before, we are deeper and richer and more fulfilled in all of our relationships.

The spiritual awakening does not lead us to reach out to others. The spiritual awakening awakens us to honesty so that we develop authentic relationships that we have not had before. We are awakened to true love with no agenda, and we learn to love well, even those who have hurt us and those whom we have hurt. And we are awakened to gratitude. We don't curse our lives; we are grateful for them and the insight we have from the pain we have endured. We live now on a spiritual plane that consists of peace and joy and serenity. We are awake to anything that might threaten our serenity or any part of this kind of life. So naturally we want to introduce others to this way of being.

We carry the message to others in many ways. One way to carry the message is to live into our recovery and restoration. When we do, people notice that we are different. They tell us they see a change because we are confident and consistent in our compassion for others. We offer to others who are suffering what we have discovered. It is not unusual for people to ask us what we have. They want to know why we are different from the way we were before and why we are different from so many others. We are so grateful for what we have found that we love to share with them how they can find it also. If they want it, we are happy to sponsor, coach, mentor, or befriend them along the way. We are messengers of hope, help, and transformation, and we love being the conduit to real change and complete restoration.

The Bible encourages us in this role of reaching out to people with a caution. We are to be humble above all else. In our humility, we are to be gentle. And we must be careful that we don't get tripped up as we are helping someone else. Here is a verse that puts it all together: "Dear brothers and sisters, if another believer is overcome by some sin, you who are godly should gently and humbly help that person back onto the right path. And be careful not to fall into the same temptation yourself" (Galatians 6:1). Humility keeps us alert to temptation and helps us avoid those situations that could take us back into our old ways. We reach out because we have been reached. We show love and offer hope in the same way we have been helped. Now pain has an amazing purpose. Life is no longer miserable as we carry out our newfound ministry, based on the home training that we did from the wounds we endured, to love well and make things right.

The most important part of Step Twelve is practicing the principles of all Twelve Steps in all of our affairs. In family, church, community, and business relationships and dealings, we know what to do, and we do it. We are honest and responsible. We reflect on and evaluate our behavior. When we are wrong, we admit it and make it right. We grow in character, and with every passing month and year, we reflect the character of God more and more. We are making progress because we identify the setbacks and set things back on the right course. We go from doing the next right thing to the next right thing, living one day at a time. We humble ourselves to see people and do what needs to be done to meet the needs of others without doing damage to ourselves. Our selfishness is behind us, and deeper and richer connections are what we seek and what fulfill us.

There are Twelve Steps, and each one holds a valuable truth that is part of transforming us. Divorce transforms us no matter what side of the conflict we are on. It is painful to us, and the collateral damage to others can be even more painful than what we go through. Transformation is what we need, and we need to continue to be transformed. When we practice the principles in all of our affairs, we never stop transforming and we never stop living in gratitude for having found the path of the Twelve Steps and the people who helped us along the way.

Step One: We must recognize our powerlessness in the unmanageability of our lives daily.

Step Two: God removes our insanity and restores our wholeness.

Step Three: We surrender to God and let go of control.

Steps Four and Five: We make an honest inventory of ourselves (not others) and share our confession with another person. We also create and share our "new normal you" inventory.

Steps Six and Seven: In humility, we seek help from God to cleanse us and fill us with new strengths.

Steps Eight and Nine: We recognize the harm we have caused to others and take action to heal our damaged relationships.

Step Ten: We continue to take inventory of our behavior, and when we are wrong, we promptly admit it.

Step Eleven: We are increasingly more conscious of God's presence.

Step Twelve: We give away what we have gained in our journey through the steps and remain in recovery in every life situation.

Practicing these principles is similar to what Jesus told his disciples: "Those who remain in me, and I in them, will produce much fruit. For apart from me you can do nothing" (John 15:5). We cannot practice the principles of the Twelve Steps without being connected to Jesus. Our priority is to apply the steps in any problem, event, situation, job, relationship, or loss—in other words, in anything that life brings to us—through the power of Jesus. When we connect to Jesus by deepening our conscious contact, he enables us to live more effectively, responsibly, and joyously.

Our shortsighted purposes for our lives begin to fade as we realize that with God's help we can conquer anything, even overcoming a painful divorce. The miracle of this partnership with God is so awe-inspiring that we are encouraged to continue recovery no matter how arduous it may be. We realize that material, worldly success pales in comparison to living vitally and purposefully. The book titled *Twelve Steps and Twelve Traditions* of Alcoholics Anonymous states, "True ambition is not what we thought it was. True ambition is the deep desire to live usefully and walk humbly under the grace of God."*

QUESTIONS FOR **STEP TWELVE**

Our Mission *Isaiah 61:1-3*

1. How have I progressed through the pain and despair of my divorce? How close am I to accepting its reality?

2. Having had a "spiritual awakening" in working these steps, how can I share my experience with others?

Our Story *Mark 16:14-18*

Describe in writing the story of your spiritual awakening and how your recovery process contributed to the awakening. Describe how you have changed.

---

* *Twelve Steps and Twelve Traditions*, (New York, NY: Alcoholics Anonymous Publishing, 1986), 124–125.

_____

_____

_____

_____

_____

_____

_____

_____

_____

_____

Persistent Prayer *Luke 11:5-10; Isaiah 52:6-7*

1. How has prayer changed for me since working the steps?

_____

_____

_____

2. What makes it difficult for me to be persistent in my praying?

_____

_____

_____

3. Have I become more interested in praying for others? Why or why not?

_____

_____

_____

Sharing Together *John 15:5-15*

1. Am I connected to the vine? How do the Twelve Steps help me to remain in him?

_____

_____

_____

2. How have the changes brought about by working the Twelve Steps made me more loving toward others?

_____

_____

_____

3. What am I doing to reach out to others with Jesus' love?

_____

_____

_____

Listening First *Acts 8:26-40*

1. What is my attitude about sharing my story of recovery? Am I reluctant to tell my story, or am I the kind of person who tends to share too much too soon with too many people?

_____

_____

_____

2. Am I willing to wait for God's timing for sharing my story?

_____

_____

_____

3. Do I see my story of recovery as valuable to God's plan for me? Describe how.

_____

_____

_____

Talking the Walk 1 Timothy 4:14-16

Paul encourages Timothy to "throw yourself into your tasks so that everyone will see your progress." What changes in my life might others observe since I have been working the Twelve Steps?

_____

_____

_____

_____

Never Forget Titus 3:1-5

What memories do I have about my old way of life? Are there any good memories? Describe some of the positive events that you want to remember.

_____

_____

_____

The Narrow Road 1 Peter 4:1-4

1. In what ways have I suffered physically for Christ in my recovery process?

_____

_____

_____

2. What do I still fear?

_____

_____

_____

_____

3. How can I work the Twelve Steps regarding this fear?

_____

_____

_____

_____

CONCLUDING THOUGHTS

Our temptation now is to think that we have finished the Twelve Steps. The reality is that the steps are never really done because we never quit growing emotionally or spiritually. By practicing the Twelve Steps, we have a path for life and a connection with God that yields greater humility and reverence for his grace and power.

You never have to wonder how to carry this message of transformation to others. It happens when you integrate the Twelve Step principles into every area of your life. You don't have to loudly proclaim the message; your changed life speaks for itself. Attending weekly meetings and working the steps are only meaningful if they result in a remarkable life that is noticeably different than before—without the same destructive habits and patterns. The message is carried further and better by a kind tongue than by articulate lips. So, carry the message of hope and transformation as you love others with all you have and all you are.

We conclude with this blessing and encouragement from Peter:

> May God give you more and more grace and peace as you grow in your knowledge of God and Jesus our Lord. By his divine power, God has given us everything we need for living a godly life. We have received all of this by coming to know him, the one who called us to himself by means of his marvelous glory and excellence. And because of his glory and excellence, he has given us great and precious promises. These are the promises that enable you to share his divine nature and escape

the world's corruption caused by human desires. In view of all this, make every effort to respond to God's promises. Supplement your faith with a generous provision of moral excellence, and moral excellence with knowledge, and knowledge with self-control, and self-control with patient endurance, and patient endurance with godliness, and godliness with brotherly affection, and brotherly affection with love for everyone. (2 Peter 1:2-7)

SCRIPTURE INDEX

Isaiah 54:4-8 Redeeming the Past
Isaiah 55:1-9 God's Abundant Pardon
Isaiah 57:12-19 Clearing the Mess
Isaiah 61:1-3 Our Mission
Jeremiah 18:1-6 Giving Up Control
Lamentations 3:17-26 God Is Faithful
Ezekiel 33:10-16 Hope for Those Making Amends
Daniel 4:19-33 Grandiose Thinking
Hosea 11:8-11 Covenant Love
Amos 7:7-8 The Plumb Line
Jonah 4:4-8 Going Deeper
Matthew 5:21-26 Handling Anger
Matthew 5:23-26 Peacemaking
Matthew 7:1-5 Finger-Pointing
Matthew 11:27-30 Submission and Rest
Matthew 13:1-23 Weeding the Garden
Matthew 16:24-26 Enjoying the Calm
Matthew 18:23-35 Forgiving Others, Forgiving Yourself
Mark 5:1-13 Internal Bondage
Mark 10:13-16 Like Little Children
Mark 16:14-18 Our Story
Luke 2:16-20 Powerful Secrets
Luke 8:43-48 Healing Faith
Luke 11:5-13 Pride Born of Hurt
Luke 11:5-10 Persistent Prayer
Luke 18:10-14 A Humble Heart
Luke 19:1-10 The Blessing of Giving
John 5:1-15 Discovering Hope
John 15:5-15 Sharing Together
Acts 8:26-40 Listening First
Acts 17:22-28 Discovering God
Romans 1:18-20 Believe
Romans 5:3-11 Rejoice Always
Romans 5:3-5 Repeated Forgiveness
Romans 8:35-39 An Overwhelming Struggle
2 Corinthians 2:5-8 Grace-Filled Living
2 Corinthians 4:7-10 The Paradox of Powerlessness
2 Corinthians 7:8-11 Constructive Sorrow
Galatians 6:9 Enjoying the Calm
Ephesians 2:8-10 A Clean Slate
Ephesians 4:26-27 Be Angry and Don't Sin

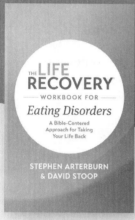
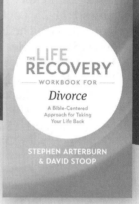
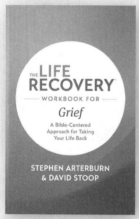
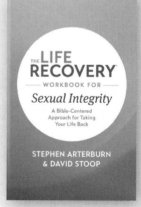